Founded 1961

North West Venturers Ya

50 years of Cruising Success

Written by Ralph Morris
with contributions from
Club members, past & present.

Published by the North West Venturers Yacht Club
Gallows Point, Beaumaris, Anglesey, LL58 8YL

First Published   2011

Printed by MWL Print Group, Pontypool
01495 750033

ISBN 978-0-9511377-5-8

Contents

Preface

Fifty years ago, on the 8th October 1961, the North West Venturers Yacht Club was formed by a small group of yachtsmen who believed that considerable cruising distances could be covered by small production yachts, provided that the boats were both adequately equipped and handled by crews who were reasonably well trained. The main objectives of the club were set and have remained unchanged over the past fifty years. They are, as originally stated in the first edition of the club newsletter *"The Venturer"* (January 1962) as: "to encourage and develop cruising in small sailing boats and the principles of navigation and seamanship."

Today the yachts may be larger with better equipment and modern navigation aids enabling greater distances to be cruised, but the crews are just as vulnerable unless they are competent to handle and navigate their craft safely. This principle is as important today as it has always been. At the time of its formation the club consisted of some ten members and four boats. Since that time it has grown to 250 members with 135 listed yachts, and is still increasing. This book covers each of the past five decades from 1961 to 2010, with information and anecdotes from the members, their yachts, cruising and racing, trophies, publications, the clubhouse and social and training activities. Not all can be covered but it does give a flavour of the Club's activities and achievements. None of these successes would have been possible without the continued enthusiasm and dedication, over the years, of the Club's Officers, Committee and Members coupled with their pride in flying the club's distinctive burgee, depicting our mermaids Ebb & Flo, who are now well recognised worldwide.

It is both a privilege and honour to introduce in this, our Golden Jubilee publication, a record of "50 years of Cruising Success".

John Partington
President

Gallows Point

The North West Venturers Yacht Club
50 years of cruising success

"The Club premises are situated on Gallows Point at the South East end of the North beach. The site is approximately 50m x 20m.

They provide a single storey building comprising galley and dining area, lounge, showers & toilets, and a lobby. A temporary steel container alongside the clubhouse provides storage for around 30 inflatables and outboard engines.

There is a patio facing Beaumaris Bay and parking space for about 25 cars in the Club's private car park to the east of the clubhouse.

It is a family oriented club, with short cruises most weekends during the season to places around the Anglesey coast. Social and training events are most prominent in the winter months, but also occur during the weekend cruises."

Ian Rodger

THIS IS THE STORY OF HOW IT CAME ABOUT.

2

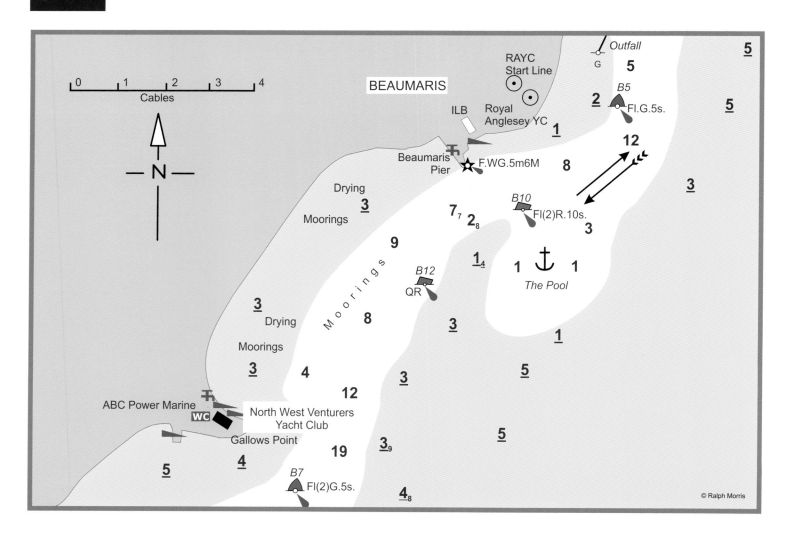

0 1 2 3 4
Cables

N

BEAUMARIS

RAYC
Start Line

Outfall
G

5

5

5

B5
Fl.G.5s.

2

ILB

Royal
Anglesey YC

1

5

Beaumaris
Pier

F.WG.5m6M

8

12

3

Drying

3

Moorings

7₇ 2₈

B10
Fl(2)R.10s.

3

9

M o o r i n g s

1₄

1 ⚓ 1

The Pool

B12
QR

8

3

3

1

3

Drying

3

Moorings

3

4

12

3

5

ABC Power Marine

WC

North West Venturers
Yacht Club

5

Gallows Point

4

19

3₉

5

5

4

B7
Fl(2)G.5s.

4₈

© Ralph Morris

The first days of the North West Venturers

Small boats had been mooring between Beaumaris Bay and the Gazelle since the 1930's, the moorings being laid in the mud of Beaumaris Bay by the boats' owners. By the late 1950's numbers had increased to a dozen or more vessels - mostly Silhouettes. By 1960 several of the yachts had been individually trailer-sailed around the coasts of Scotland, Wales, (southern) England and the North coast of France.

It was time for a cruise in company. The North West Silhouette Owners Association organised a trip to the Isle of Man in the summer of 1961 and a few of the Strait's other inhabitants travelled with them, making nine boats in all. These included Don McKnight and his wife of a few days, Hilary, honeymooning in a 19ft Caprice! (See Appendix III for details of the cruise)

Huddled together against the island's typically welcoming weather systems, the skippers began to form the idea of a club, based in Beaumaris, and open to every type of sailing boat.

On their return they developed the concept and, on 8th October 1961, at a meeting in the Blossoms Hotel, Chester **the North West Venturers Yacht Club was born.**

Honeymoon Cruise Ship to IoM

Photo: Don & Hilary McKnight

By the start of 1962 the Club gave every impression of being fully established.

A competition was held to design a burgee and Storm Bate was the worthy (*sic!*) winner. (From

the beginning a majority the Club's membership has been endowed with a healthily irreverent sense of humour). Ebb & Flo became the symbol of the Club's attitude to living, though their originally over-developed bosoms were substantially reduced in size before the burgees were produced.

Members' senses of humour weren't THAT irreverent!

Coupled with this zest for fun came a powerful sense of responsibility and awareness of the risks of offshore sailing. Cruising in company was the most obvious demonstration of this, and by January 1962 plans were in train for cruises to both Ireland and Scotland with another mooted for France, starting from the South Coast.

All of this in yachts of less than 24ft LoA. No VHF radios, no RDF beacons, no self steering.

The Club's first Newsletter appeared in January 1962, just three months after the formation of the Club with a Who's Who of the founder members (see p7) and news of its first trophies:

- *"The Walton Shield" presented by Geoff Walton for the "Senior Race" - a race of 25nm or longer.*
- *"The Storm Cup" presented by Storm Bate for a Cruising Log.*

Wilf Jacques also offered a "Clot's Cup" for the biggest clot of the season, though the definition of a clot was left to the imagination.

Other forms of racing were also not neglected, with a decision to have a Points Trophy for the winner of a series of six races and another race to Ten Feet Bank buoy. Members were asked if they would like to donate a trophy.

Club premises were already being discussed, with the commodore's garage attic acting as temporary accommodation. This first newsletter asked for contributions to furnish it - blankets being high on the list!

As the anonymous editor of the NWVYC's first ever **Venturer** wrote:

Continued on Page 6

The Founders

As described in the Club's first newsletter (January 1962)

Commodore	Judge Meurig Evans	*"Maid of Skye" (Hillyard). A deep sea type with a weakness for keeping a weather eye on twin keel inexperienced sailors.*
Vice-commodore	Storm Bate	*"Eileen" (Leeward). Quiet & unassuming. Often mistaken for a Breton onion-seller.*
Rear-commodore	Geoff Walton	*"Pandora" (Nobby). If you ever find Geoff not smiling or helping somebody, you are having delusions. Knows the Strait like the back of his hand.*
Secretary	Wilfred Jacques	*"Karena" (Mystic). Iron Man. Famed for his excellent mime - or maybe he just talks more slowly than he mimes.*
	Patricia Bate	*Should have been christened Patience. She needs it!*
	Patricia Walton	*Hopes to sail in the Nobby this year. Always makes you welcome at Appletree Cottage.*
	Connie Jacques	*Dark haired sylph.*
	David & Barbara Cooke	*Like big engines and anchoring on concrete slipways!*
	Michael & Margit Hardman	*Moors his Nobby by the Gazelle to be sure to sleep aboard instead of hoping the weather suggests a night ashore.*
	William Locke	*Convinced his Wavecrest has all the advantages of a cruiser with the speed of a dinghy.*
	Jim & Audrey Berry	*Sailed to the IoM last year in a leaking Caprice. Changing his boat this year.*
	Don McKnight	*"Sanpan" (Caprice). Only man to sail to the IoM without a male crew - but he was on his honeymoon!*
	Roy Wooler	*Sails a Silhouette and a Princess, both designed by Bob Tucker. He sails from Conway in all sorts of weather.*

```
┌─────────────────────────────────────────────┐
│  ─── T H E   V E N T U R E R ───              │
│                                               │
│                          January 1962         │
│                                               │
│  *** COMMODORE'S LETTER ***                    │
│                                               │
│  TO THE OFFICERS AND MEMBERS OF THE NORTH WEST VENTURERS CLUB. │
│                                               │
│     THIS CLUB OF WHICH I AM MOST PROUD TO BE THE FIRST COMMODORE, │
│  OWES ITS ORIGIN TO THE URGE FELT BY SOME MEMBERS OF THE NORTH WEST │
│  SILHOUETTE OWNERS ASSOCIATION TO CATER FOR SAILING ACTIVITIES WHICH │
│  ARE NOT RESTRICTED TO ANY ONE CLASS BOAT. AT THE SAME TIME IT WAS │
│  FELT DESIRABLE THAT OWNERS AND CREWS OF THE MISCELLANEOUS TYPES OF │
│  SMALL CRUISING BOATS, NOW BECOMING MORE AND MORE POPULAR, SHOULD │
│  HAVE GREATER OPPORTUNITY OF TAKING PART IN ORGANISED CRUISES IN │
│  COMPANY ONE WITH ANOTHER. │
│     LAST YEARS ISLE OF MAN CRUISE ORGANISED BY THE OFFICERS OF THE │
│  SILHOUETTE ASSOCIATION WAS A GOOD EXAMPLE WHICH WE HOPE WILL PROVE │
│  BUT THE FIRST OF MANY OF ITS KIND. THAT CRUISE DEMONSTRATED AMONG │
│  SEVERAL OTHER THINGS,THAT OFF-SHORE SAILING,IF IT IS TO BE ENJOYED │
│  TO THE FULL, DEMANDS SOMETHING MORE THAN A MERE CAPACITY TO SAIL A │
│  BOAT IN SHELTERED WATERS FROM ONE POINT TO ANOTHER IN THE SHORTEST │
│  POSSIBLE TIME. IT DEMANDS NOT ONLY A THOROUGH KNOWLEDGE OF ONE'S │
│  BOAT, BUT PAINSTAKING CARE TO ENSURE THAT ALL ITS PARTS AND EQUIP- │
│  MENT ARE SOUND AND IN GOOD ORDER AND CONDITION. IT CALLS FOR SOME │
│  KNOWLEDGE OF PRACTICAL SEAMANSHIP, AND OF PILOTAGE AND COASTAL │
│  NAVIGATION - HOW TO RECOGNISE THE DIFFERENT KINDS OF BUOYS AND │
│  LIGHTS, TO KNOW ABOUT TIDES AND TO MAKE THE BEST USE OF THEM, TO │
│  LEARN TO AVOID THE DANGERS OF THE COAST, AND TO ENSURE AS FAR AS │
│  KNOWLEDGE AND CARE CAN DO SO, THAT WE MAKE SAFE AND HAPPY LANDINGS │
│  AT OUR CHOSEN DESTINATION. │
│     HOWEVER GOOD A BOAT MAY BE, SHE IS NO BETTER THAN THE MEN - AND │
│  WOMEN - WHO SAIL IN HER. IT IS THE HUMAN FACTOR THAT IS OF PARA- │
│  MOUNT IMPORTANCE IN SAILING AND PARTICULARLY IN CRUISING. THE SEA │
│  IS DANGEROUS, TREACHEROUS AND UNCERTAIN. BUT MAN IS A SENTIENT │
│  ENTITY,AND EQUIPPED WITH INTELLIGENCE,KNOWLEDGE AND DETERMINATION. │
│  HE CAN ENDOW HIS BOAT WITH THESE QUALITIES SO THAT A SEAMAN AND │
│  HIS BOAT BECOME AS ONE, EACH DEPENDENT ON AND WITH CONFIDENCE IN │
│  THE OTHER. │
│     ACCORDINGLY I WOULD LIKE, AS COMMODORE, TO FEEL THAT THOSE WHO │
│  SAIL UNDER THE VENTURERS FLAG, SET AN EXAMPLE IN THIS RESPECT BY │
│  THE CARE AND PRIDE THEY TAKE IN THEIR BOATS AND IN THE HANDLING OF │
│  THEM, AND BY THE RESPECT THEY PAY TO THE SEA AND ALL ITS WAYS. │
│                                      MEURIG EVANS │
│                                       COMMODORE │
└─────────────────────────────────────────────┘
```

Continued from page 4

"The spirit of adventure, the physical effort leading to fulfilment of purpose, the satisfaction of a landfall or port made after a tedious passage, this is the medium in which we deal".

Thus, by the end of 1961, the North West Venturers Yacht Club had a membership of ten plus yachts. By the start of the 1962 season, this had risen to nineteen boats.

The First Year of Cruising (1962)

The Venturers started as they were to continue - watching the boats heaving at their chains from the misery of the beach, the shelter of The Judge's garage or the comfort of the Gazelle Hotel. A cruise to Caernarfon in May was somewhat influenced by a SW8-9, a trip to Rhyl was curtailed by a forecast of SW8. By the time of the Whitsun Bank Holiday, the Programme was decimated, and Wilf Jacques & Storm Bate substituted Port St Mary for Dun Laoghaire in a forecast SW3 veering NW3, with every expectation of a fine sail.

They left the Gazelle at 1530hrs. By 2300hrs (LW) they were abeam Point Lynas in a N5-6 and determined to return to the planned cruise destination - Dun Laoghaire. Off the Skerries against a flood tide by 0500hrs, they decided to curtail the cruise by heading into Holyhead, where they arrived by 0700hrs. Clearly Ireland was off the menu if they were to be back at work on Tuesday - so they completed the first circumnavigation of the Island. For this feat, the Club struck a "Round the Island" pennant. By the end of the season they had been joined by nine other members including John Law in 'El Lobo' who wondered if he qualified since he had included Conwy and the Isle of Man in the circumnavigation.

Undaunted by the season's progress, three club boats (a Leeward, a Mystic and a Caprice) all around 20ft in length, were trailed to Weymouth early in August for a cruise to the Channel Islands and Cherbourg. As Storm Bate put it, "We learnt a great deal from this cruise and proved a number of things, mostly about our own endurance powers, taking the helm for 16 to 18 hours. This was felt to be a bit much ...".

"Maid of Skye"

PHOTO: Don McKnight

His Log of the cruise won the new trophy for a long cruise - the "Commodore's Cup".

Another two trophies had been donated by the time the season started. "The Venturers Cup" by Arthur Goodwin (universally known as 'Goody' - even in the committee Minutes!) for a combination of seamanship and quality of cruising Log and the "Astrador Boats Cup", later to be truncated to the "Astrador Cup" by Astrador Boats of Manchester. It carried with it an award of a 10 guinea voucher to be exchanged at Astrador Boats and was to be awarded to the winner of a Round Anglesey race. It too fell foul of the weather. 'Goody' also donated the "Irene Goodwin Trophy" in tribute to his wife who would patiently sit in their car while he went sailing. With typical Venturers' humour, the Irene Goodwin race required wives to helm.

This first season's weather, though nothing special for the Menai Strait ("gales devastated the programme") concentrated attention on a key element of sailing - staying dry! Minds became focussed on club premises.

The Clubhouse

By 1963 the novelty of the Judge's garage was wearing off and, even though it had gained

'Venturers' in Port St Mary

Photo: Don McKnight

camp beds, chairs and even electricity, the ground swell for something different was growing.

The Gazelle Hotel at Glyngarth became the effective headquarters of the Club but with nearly seventy members it quickly became clear that a clubhouse was a necessity.

Options to rent a building on Beaumaris Pier, snug down in the Pendyffryn Country Club, buy a cottage, a hulk, a caravan or even a fudge factory were considered and rejected. Negotiations were opened by the indefatigable Storm Bate with Beaumaris council and the county council (Anglesey) for a lease on a piece of land at Gallows Point. A proposition was put to an Extraordinary General Meeting on 10th April 1963. The lease was be at an annual rate of 1d per square foot for the land and an extra ½d per sq.ft. for the Clubhouse itself.

Mssrs John Osola, Don McKnight, Jim Berry and Ian Warren (the Club architect, without whose influence the Clubhouse may have looked very different) estimated that a 30ft by 18ft building could be erected for £1400, if the final fitting out was done by club members.

Twenty six members attended the meeting. Twenty six members voted in favour. Within a month or so the full amount had been raised through donations, loans and guarantees.

Until the clubhouse was built, Morris & Leavett (later to become ABC Boatyard) gave club members access to their toilets! Antlers (still on the Lounge wall) were salvaged from a fund raising Jumble Sale, to provide a hat stand and the foundations were in place by the end of June. By mid-August the building was finished, just about the time that Beaumaris Pier was demolished in preparation for its reconstruction.

The Clubhouse arrives!

Photo: Don McKnight

By the time of the AGM in November, the essentials were all but finished and the search was on for suitable photographs to break the monotony of the pristine white walls. As John Osola wrote in the December 1963 newsletter "Full plate enlargements of members' boats are now urgently required".

The Clubhouse opening was widely reported in the local press and yachting magazines - the Venturers were famous! The mayor & mayoress of Beaumaris (Councillor & Mrs J G Dixon) officially opened the premises on Saturday 11th April 1964. Later in 1964 the Club appointed its first "Club Warden" - Joyce Swinton.

Over the years the Clubhouse has been granted additional leases and has subsequently been further extended with the help of additional donations and guarantees from members and grants from sports funding bodies.

In 2010 plans were being drawn up for a new building to replace the existing one - and the lease was once again being negotiated with the council. This time at least a 99 year lease is the target.

Clubhouse - 1964

Photos: Don & Hilary McKnight

CLUBHOUSE OPENING

Top Left: Clubhouse
Left: Christine Osola presents the mayoress with a bouquet, watched by the commodore.
Top right: members wait patiently with the food.
Bottom right: The panoramic windows.

Training

The early members could see the reputation of the Club growing rapidly and were determined that the Club would become an exemplar for cruiser sailing.

The Hon. Training Officer role was embedded in the first draft of a Constitution, which included in its Objectives "... the study of the principles of navigation and seamanship". Geoff Walton was appointed the Club's first Hon. Training Officer, a role which appeared before Secretary and Treasurer in the Club's documentation and it was not long before Training cruises and Winter Training evenings were appearing in the Programme.

By 1964 articles on navigation, passage planning - and man overboard procedures - were rife in the Club Newsletter/Journal and Winter meetings were launched, typically in a Chester Hotel, to present navigation theory, plan next year's cruise and taste wine. The wine tasting usually took place around a talk by some famous person or potential sponsor.

When the Welsh Yachting Association (WYA) was formed as the Royal Yachting Association's (RYA) administrative branch for Wales, the Club was one of the first to lend its support. Training Officer Arthur Birtwistle enrolled 23 members on the RYA Offshore Certificate and reported that "the number of members owning sextants has increased greatly". He also persuaded the RYA to delete the swimming requirement from the course syllabus, allowing Club members to drown without reproach.

In time, the RYA changed its policies and withdrew its license to grant certificates from all sailing clubs. But NWVYC did not stop training - it just changed its nature. Winter evenings in assorted hotels addressed engine servicing, First Aid (including time spent with Dr John Bennett's doll), Aids to Navigation, from celestial navigation to satellite navigation, and "Defensive Passage Planning". Defensive planning being preparation of a passage plan which included chartage for all the bolt holes which might conceivably be needed if things went wrong.

By the mid-1970s the Club was training with Beaumaris RNLI

Beaumaris Lifeboat circa 1965

Photo: RNLI

(then with a Watson class offshore boat housed in Friars Bay) and the SAR helicopter service from RAF Valley. The relationship has remained strong since those days and in 2010 several Club members are actively involved in running the Beaumaris lifeboat.

Formal training declined as more and more emphasis was placed on events such as the RNLI training days. "First trip through the Swellies" appeared on the Programme, under the guidance of the Training Officer, 'Survival Technique' days

Silhouettes in Beaumaris Bay

were arranged at local swimming pools and, by the 1990s the Club was liaising with colleges running RYA courses to give students a taste of real sailing. 1994 saw the Club's 'victims' get more of an engorgement than a taste! More of that later as "The Great Conwy Gale".

The final death knoll of the formal Training Officer role came with the galloping intrusion of Health & Safety and the litigious society of the late 1990s. It became just too expensive to insure ourselves. To make sure that Training wasn't forgotten, the role was integrated into a new position of Sailing captain; which is where it remains today.

But, training has always been there for a purpose, to help members keep their focus firmly fixed on safe cruising - particularly the longer distance cruises to Isle of Man, Ireland, Brittany, the Mediterranean and beyond. The cry "Arthur Birtwistle says ... " can still be heard whenever seamanship is being debated by Venturers.

Today, the Club again holds an RYA Training Centre licence, thanks to Derek Lumb who became its first 21st century "Principal".

The rest of the Sixties

1965 started auspiciously with Ebb & Flo being exhibited on the RYA stand at the Earls Court Boat Show and a Cheese & Wine Tasting party in February. This set the standard for Venturer intoxication with over 100 folk dispatching some 70 bottles of quality wine and about 30 lbs of assorted cheeses. It added £30 3s. 8d to the Club funds.

The Spring Newsletter/Journal (the Club had still to decide what to publish and how to publish it) detailed the membership as it was after only three seasons in existence. Eighty eight fully paid up members plus assorted offspring (at 5 guineas per Family membership).

By start of season this had increased to 112 members attached to sixty one boats of which 19 were Silhouettes. Many of the boats still maintained moorings off the Gazelle, but the proximity of Beaumaris Bay to the Clubhouse, and the recent acquisition of Peter Brimecombe (soon to become Moorings contractor par excellence) meant that members with bilge-keelers were slowly migrating to the Bay's mud.

In those days many moorings were positioned in the Bay by being thrown over the side in the boatowner's favourite spot, not always clear of tackle left behind by the guy who got there first last year! The Club owned a number of moorings off the Gazelle Hotel which were leased to members and maintained by Emlyn Oliver. And Club boats were increasing in size with a number of REALLY BIG yachts of over 25ft.

With all this activity the Beaumaris Council just had to see an opportunity and in 1966 mooring owners were presented with a contract and a bill. The Club's legal eagle, Dickie Roper, could not see much of a legal case against charging fees above the LW mark but it was an entirely different matter in the deep. He and Peter Brimecombe set themselves a mission with the council which only ended in 1969 when an 'equitable' arrangement was reached. That year, everybody paid:

- *3s per foot per year for vessels less than 25ft.*
- *4s per foot per year for vessels over 25ft.*

'Sampan' in the Strait
Photo: Don McKnight

On other fronts, the Club and Beaumaris Council got along well. The council saw the income and prestige that the Club was bringing to the town and was keen to see it develop. In 1967 the Clubhouse lease was extended to incorporate more land. Discussions started for an extension to a building on which the paint was hardly dry with rumblings about workshops, dinghy stores and car parks.

Afloat, seventeen club boats entered the Astrador Boat Round Anglesey race in 1966, which was already becoming a two part event. Leg One to Holyhead, Leg 2 (the following day) back to the Start Line. By 1968, the second leg of the race had been dropped.

The Start Line was also on the move. Whilst a casual start in the region of the Gazelle was acceptable to the earliest members, it was felt that a Club of some 120 members (it seemed to grow daily!) needed a proper Start/Finish line. A red triangle was bolted onto the flagstaff and one of the duties of the Officer of the Day (OoD) was to erect an outer marker on the promenade. It wasn't long before this was seen as unwarranted discrimination against fin-keelers which had a tendency to ground before they could finish a race. Whilst some felt that this was a perfectly fair handicap for fin-keelers, others believed that this was taking officialdom at NWVYC races a touch too far. It was determined that "roughly about here" would suffice for both

TROPHIES (1968)

Commodore's Cup	Presented by Judge Evans for best Log of cruise of more than 100nm. (Senior Log competition).
Storm Trophy	Presented by Storm Bate for best Log of cruise of less than 100nm. (Junior Log competition).
Venturers' Cup	Presented by 'Goody' Goodwin. Awarded by Officers to any member for a feat justifying particular recognition.
Firth Trophy	Winner of first points race of the season.
Astrador Cup	Winner on handicap to first Venturer to finish in MCA Jubilee Cup race from Puffin to Holyhead.
Walton Shield	Winner of Senior Trophy Race, longer than normal and requiring navigational ability as well as speed.
James Berry Trophy	Winner of single handed race including circumnavigation of Puffin Island.
Irene Goodwin Cup	Winner of Ladies race, open only to craft helmed by ladies. Donated by 'Goody' Goodwin.
Points Trophy	Presented by John Osola for best record in Club races.

Start and Finish Outer Markers and the club drove ahead to many years of keenly contested, but informal, racing. Entirely in accord with the Club spirit, an Eight Hour Race was introduced in 1969. The rules for this race quoted turning marks such as "6 cables off Lynas lighthouse, bearing 225°M". It would be a further 40 years before any Venturer could, with certainly, say that they were 6 ca off Lynas lighthouse, bearing 225°M - and even then the °M might give some trouble!

In a hugely complex calculation, which saw the Club using computers for the very first time, the first Eight Hour Race was won by Chris Hind with 31.5 corrected miles.

But the Club's primary interest has always been cruising, near and far, with an element of competition visible in most undertakings. Entries into the Log competitions also contained such repetitive phrases as "As usual we were late..."; "unexpectedly the tide was against us...", "otherwise it would have been quite a pleasant harbour", often written by the "crew, foredeck hand, helm, food procurer, cook, stout drinker". Yes - whatever the claims, it was often the womenfolk (invariably wives in those days) who made it happen!

A theme which developed in this period and which has persisted to the present day is encapsulated in the phrase "... the programme was devastated by the weather ..." This resulted in the Club's first helicopter rescue (1967) when a Club boat became embayed in Cemaes Bay. The crew was airlifted to safety and the yacht was towed to Holyhead by the Holyhead lifeboat. Despite the weather, Club boats cruised some way from home shores and in 1969 the Club published a guide to well known clubs, complete with local facilities and engine agents. These included:

- Holyhead SC
- Pwllheli SC
- Manx Sailing & Cruising Club, Ramsey
- Isle of Man Yacht Club, Port St Mary
- Down Cruising Club, Strangford Lough
- Strangford Lough YC
- Carlingford Lough YC
- Royal Irish YC, Dun Laoghaire
- Royal St George YC, Dun Laoghaire
- Kinsale YC
- Baltimore SC

PRESIDENT

At the AGM of 1966, Judge Meurig Evans was elected as the Club's first President. He was to hold the position for life - or until he felt he had had enough.

But even this failed to fully represent the achievements of the Venturers of the 1960's, because Cherbourg isn't listed - where the Robertshaw's went on their delivery trip from Littlehampton with Macwester No. 59. Nor is Loch Fyne included, where Arthur Birtwistle took his 16 ft Wavecrest with son Philip. Mind you, he did trail it to Greenock. Nor should John Law's harbours of St Mary's (Scilly Isles), Rosslare and Arklow be omitted when he took his Eventide 'El Lobo' for a fortnight's summer cruise.

The social calendar had been well established from the earliest days of the Club. Usually held in

the Chester/Liverpool/ Manchester triangle, events sometimes masqueraded as a Training session, sometimes an erudite tale of lessons learnt on a cruise (which could also be construed as training). In 1969, Ye Angel Hotel in Knutsford was the regular venue. The annual dinner/dance took place at the Manor Hey Hotel in Urmston: *"Starting gun 1930 hours for Dinner at 2000. The cost of tickets will be 2guineas per head"* ... *"Following the derogatory remarks of some of the "younger" members upon the beat capabilities of the Palm Court Orchestra, Bryan Hopton has been persuaded to seek-out and engage some sort of foil to the resident band"*

The end of the decade was marked by a beach bonfire party and an exhortation to use up old flares by firing them off alongside the fireworks. Firing off old flares was encouraged by the coastguard as a common sense means of both disposing of them and gaining valuable experience. The days of political correctness had yet to cast their dark shadow on the Club.

By 2010 the good days were over and Club fireworks *displays* finally surrendered to pressure from the Health & Safety types, reinforced by insurance premium demands.

The Seventies

The Boat builders

If the 1960's were marked by building a Club, the seventies was a period of building boats. The first to start the progression to larger DIY yachts was John Law. His 38ft (some reports say it was 40ft) C-bird concrete yacht was underway by January 1970. In true Venturer style the build was well reported in the press, none more expansively than in the 'Steel News' - "The high tensile reinforcing rod and half inch water piping was lashed together with 16 gauge Rylands and covered with eight layers of wire mesh, laced to the frame with 19 gauge tying wire. Fifteen rolls of 22 gauge mesh were needed, costing £150". Yeah, OK - but it also made a very solid yacht.

John, a Manchester Ship Canal pilot, planned to be one of the Club's first transatlantic venturers. In the event he was beaten to it by David & Clare Price and family in 'Domino'. No doubt motivated by John's good progress during the year, five other members started home build jobs and by the time he launched in October 1971 a total of ten projects were under way. The latest starts were Ted Hobart's Norwest 34, 'Nauphante' and Donald Shelley's Hustler 30.

David Swinton fitted out the first home-built Macwester in his garden, though by the time it was finished there were ribald comments about his new garden shed; Vic Donnelly built first

John Law and "El Lobo"

Photo: Steel News

Seamint leaves home

PHOTO: Gordon Rutter

his Halcyon 23, then under pressure from Hazel and family, upsized to a Norwest 34 (somewhat in advance of Ted Hobart's); Paddy Sanday fitted out his Trident, the Twemlow's went upmarket for an Olsen 38 - and Gordon & Marjorie Rutter followed

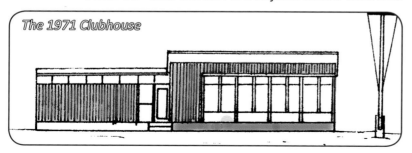

The 1971 Clubhouse

John Law with a concrete hull. 'Seamint' took over their back garden in 1973 and was craned out over the house in 1976. Roy Francis started on his Seadog "Restless".

The Club has always had more than its fair share of self-build members: Jerry Lomas, John Partington, Brian Parr, Brian Butterworth, Phil Orr, and Peter Brimecombe, and undoubtedly others who have kept their skills secret, perhaps in case they were called upon to build a new Clubhouse. The builds were in steel, concrete and fibreglass. Peter Brimecombe, though concentrated on traditional wood and made a business of it.

Spurred by the enthusiasm of the DIY builders the Club took on more extensions in 1971 - ten years after the Club was founded and only seven years after the Clubhouse was built. The Changing Rooms constructed then are still in use on the Club's Fiftieth Anniversary - though like grandfather's hammer, most bits have been replaced over the years. There was much debate at the time as to whether ladies would actually want to shower!

About the same time that the changing rooms were proposed, developers had requested planning permission to build apartments on Gallows Point.

This delayed construction of the extension until the council had dispatched the developers - February 1971 , but only after much controversy and a Public Enquiry.

That was nothing to the controversy generated by the Isle of Man government's declaration of harbour dues! Members usually moored free where-ever they went and objected strenuously to formalised berthing charges. The Club made the newspapers when they cancelled their 1972 cruise to the island in protest. The protest was effective because, the following year, the IoM government reduced their harbour fees. The Club was able to re-instate its summer cruise through the Island to Scotland, with some boats now using the new-fangled Radio Direction Finders (RDF - licences £2.50p).

Despite the fact that we were now entering the Winter of Discontent and petrol was scarce, training sessions continued in Altrincham (or Knutsford) hotels with RYA certificates the goal. The club had been one of the first yacht clubs to join the Welsh Yachting Association which was, in those days, seen to be making strenuous efforts to support the cruiser sailor. It was a couple of decades later

that the Club relinquished its association as a result of the stance the WYA was then taking to cruising.

Aids to Navigation

The '70's saw momentous developments in Aids to Navigation. The RDF became standard on all boats (though few skippers admitted knowing that they should be paying a licence fee) and by the latter part of the decade, most yachts also carried VHF radios (with the same level of awareness of licence fees!). The Seavoice RT100 was universal equipment and a 'Club Channel' was agreed so that everybody would have the appropriate crystals fitted.

With the Seavoice VHF came the Seafix RDF. A short rod aerial enabled the user to find a null point, when the kit was pointing directly at the beacon. Within twenty minutes most crew had found three nulls and were able to construct a cocked hat on the chart. Sometimes, the fix was accurate to within a square mile! A major improvement on Dead Reckoning with a trailing log. Cries of "It's not like it used to be" began to echo around the moorings.

Others took advantage of this "stress-free" navigation, took their sextants out of their boxes and declared the 1973 Summer Cruise for Belle Isle. Those who could not spare three (3) weeks to go to the Morbihan (and back) settled for Southern Ireland or Northern Scotland.

And still the membership increased. By the mid-1970s the Club had more than 150 members and eighty boats (the discrepancy in numbers being a tendency to count 'Family' members as TWO. They were at least that, and frequently many more, and increasing, as children arrived. Space again became a problem in the Clubhouse, somewhat alleviated by a substantial galley make-over in the middle of the 1976 season.

As a result of growth in members new to sailing, navigation beyond the changing rooms, even over the short distance to Holyhead, became an issue. The Isle of Man was a serious venture for some 50% of Club members.

Dr Robert Kemp published his "Irish Sea Cruising Guide" in 1976, prompting the Club to commission Arthur Birtwistle, George Driver and Ken Unsworth to produce a three part pilot to Anglesey. Parts 1 & 2 were published in 1978 but Part Three never quite made it to the printers. It was the absence of this North and East coast guide which prompted Ralph Morris to write the current 'Cruising Anglesey' pilot (of which more later).

By the end of the decade, the Yearbook (or 'Blue Book' as it was called) showed the Club with 214 members owning 96 boats. The Club was finding it increasingly difficult to keep in touch with everyone.

Communicating with the membership

Over 200 members took some communicating with and long suffering Hon Secretary Ken Unsworth produced over 70 issues of *the Venturer* in ten years. Typewritten (with the aid of Snopake!), hand collated, folded, enveloped and posted, he published not only letters from escapees to warmer shores but Logs, cruise reports, training materials (including a lengthy paper complete with diagrams on the use of RDF beacons by John Bennett) and even a regular Cooking Corner for those longer passages. It was during the 1970's that *the Venturer* became an indispensable part of the Club's ethos.

In the first few years of existence membership had been small enough to get along without any formal means of communication. True, the first *Venturer* had been published in January 1962, with No.5 being reached by August 1963. Then its format changed. A stapled A5 booklet became a roneo-d broadsheet and *the Venturer* became the title of the club's Journal - Logs, erudite articles and policy statements; a glossy cover and a cover price of 5/-. By 1970, the (approximately) monthly newspaper had grown a cover sheet and under Ken Unsworth's tutelage, dealt with anything and everything about the Club: except the Constitution and Membership List which became the Yearbook in 1982.

Through the ensuing decades, *the Venturer* has remained the primary means of communication between members and the Club's hierarchy. From reports of cruises to changes in the fuel laws, from 'confessionals' to engine servicing, the newsletter has covered most subjects of interest to the cruising yachtsman.

With eight issues (or thereabouts) each year, the newsletter was able to advertise forthcoming events (including additions to members' families!), boat show trips and memorabilia - for sale through the Club's Bosun's Store. It has changed editor many times and with each change there has been a change in emphasis and content; the present style was established by Ian Rodger when he took over in 1993. He transferred production to his PC and a local printer. Advances in desk top publishing allowed his successor, Ralph Morris, to explore more adventurous layouts, whilst his successor, Carolyn Warburton added colour and a link to the club web site.

Some editors had a less reverent sense of humour than others and it had its fair share of controversial articles. As one editor put it "If 10% of the members don't find something to complain about, it's not interesting enough". Rock Trophy poems came high on the controversy list.

Around the turn of the century, the Club branched out into the Internet with a web site which has twice been awarded the accolade of "one of the best sailing club sites to be found" by the yachting press (once for each of its webmasters).

1979

Nineteen seventy nine was a special year in many ways.

On the cruising front, not many Club boats went very far. The year started with a storm at Gallows Point which blew over a number of boats, including Eric Cross' 'Swn-y-Mor', the most sailed and cosseted boat in the Club. Eric had been afloat for more than 100 days in the previous year.

Then we heard about the death, in a car accident, of Dick Partington. Dick had been the first club member to go to St. Kilda - perhaps it would be more accurate to say, achieve the goal of St. Kilda. Fifty miles into the North Atlantic from the Sound of Harris, and three hundred miles from Anglesey, St. Kilda is a destination that Venturers have aspired to since the Club was formed. In commemoration, the Club forged the St. Kilda Trophy, a plaque secured in the Clubhouse with the names of every member who has been to St Kilda. (See Appendix II).

Fastnet Race
Photo: Unknown

Then there was the infamous Fastnet Race. No Club boats were lost, but a number of members became entangled in the weather systems during their cruises and delivery trips.

The year also saw the introduction of the cardinal system of buoyage and consequential need to buy new charts ahead of plan - though for some Venturers 'plan' meant "around the turn of the century"! Such members were considerably helped by the UKHOs introduction of the Small Craft Notices to Mariners. These quarterly publications filtered the daily Notices to Mariners to leave only those Notices of interest to small craft and made a huge difference to those members who kept their charts up to date.

Then, in August, the council presented its proposals to develop Gallows Point. The Club was heartened by statements such as "...will continue to be associated with sailing and boating" and "restrain overly commercial aspects". It was less enthusiastic about "... with the proposed rent increases the total income could be increased by over 250%".

It never happened, though proposals to "improve" Gallows Point have been tabled several times since.

The Eighties

After two decades of outstanding growth, serious venturing and extensive building it was time for a period of consolidation. The Club produced its own Log Book to help those who sailed the British Isles and published a continual stream of letters from Venturers in the Mediterranean, West Indies, Azores, Spain and France. The Pilot was published midway through the decade.

Differences with the Manx government had been settled with some very reasonable harbour dues and a 10% discount had been negotiated with Manx Knitwear. Whilst on the topic of money, the very first newsletters of the decade maintained a theme established at least ten years earlier:- "The treasurer would be very pleased to receive your subscriptions ...".

One aspect of the Club which grew even more dramatically during the early part of the eighties was the (Summer) cruise in company. The benefits of having assistance nearby were amply illustrated every year. *"Sankevic radioed that the fuel line had fractured, so he was taken in tow by Shirlena while Vic on Settler turned a new olive and Gordon*

(Seamint) annealed the pipe". Then there was *W.J Kay* (Des Booth) whose stern shaft came loose north of Ardnamurchen and was towed by five other Club boats to Loch Melfort for repairs. And there were many other instances where sailing in company saved the day.

Together, Club boats headed for the Hebrides each July - sometimes being allowed by the weather

St Kilda

Photo: Gordon Rutter

to get as far as the Isle of Man, sometimes making it to the elusive St. Kilda. In the case of Geoff & Vera Schofield in 'Solitaire', only after nine attempts. They eventually got there with 'Seamint' in 1988.

The Club also had its share of excitement closer to home. In an early season cruise to Holyhead (1981) 'Robaine', a mile ahead of the fleet, was knocked down by a sudden squall, recovered and warned the others. By the time equilibrium was re-established and masts counted, Ron Leighton and family (with St Bernard dog) in their 22ft Seal 'La Orquidea' had disappeared from view. After a full scale coastguard & lifeboat search they were spotted in Holyhead harbour by our own Arthur Birtwistle. Without a VHF radio they had simply kept going into a northerly 8-9! They did say that they hoped all cruises weren't so wet - and they got a little concerned when water flowed into the cabin. They bought a VHF set the following week.

The Rock Trophy

PHOTO: Paul Wolf

Five years later the fleet was drifting towards Caernarfon Bar in the Walton Shield race when Hurricane Charlie was announced on TV. Yachts were sunk on their moorings

> VHF became essential equipment by the mid-80s and Anglesey Radio was launched by the BT (or was it still GPO?) to offer a telephone service to mariners.

throughout the Irish Sea. Lesser disasters beset Club boats in sight of the Clubhouse - and John Bennett presented the Rock Trophy to the Club.

Rock Trophy

John Bennett had a well deserved reputation for searching for eddies close inshore. This frequently resulted in 'Shirlena', a Westerly Berwick, making contact with the ground. It's a tribute to the quality of the boat build that no permanent damage was caused. So well known were his exploits in both 'Shirlena' and his subsequent yacht 'Avilion' (an Excalibur 36) that an Anonymous contributor to the Venturer somewhat controversially wrote:

> "If you can see Avilion underway then there are no rocks in the neighbourhood.

> "If you can see Avilion stationary then there are rocks in the neighbourhood."

One weekend, digging in his garden, John found a cannon ball and in an inspired moment (no doubt thinking about the state of his keel as he viewed the dents in the cannon ball) he conceived a trophy for "the club member who makes most impact on an underwater object". It's first recipient was Bernie Hobart on 'Nauphante' who berthed himself on 'Maen Piscar', one of the island's best known, but unmarked, drying rocks.

Its award has always been in the grant of the current holder, who will often spend his year buying information about Club members who may have faltered. In 1987, John Powell, in awarding the trophy to Gordon Rutter, started the tradition of writing a poem (See Appendix V). This also started the tradition of finding as many potential recipients as possible, exposing all, but reserving the trophy for one final victim. However, the thought of having to write a poem has probably been a greater motivator to avoid the award than any determination to avoid rocks.

Some members have received the trophy with pride, others have gone to extraordinary lengths to avoid mention. Whatever the reaction, the Rock Trophy has been awarded to somebody every year from its inception to today. The 2010 'winners' have the dubious honour of being recorded for posterity in this Anniversary book - they are the joint owners of 'Hwyl Dda', Malcolm & Shona Thomas and Nick & Julie Lowther.

> Judge David Meurig Evans, the Club's first Commodore and President, died peacefully at home on 7th March 1983.

Racing

This was also the decade of Club races. Members have always been ambivalent in their approach to racing. In public, racing was frequently derided - but whenever another sail was visible above the horizon sails were finely tuned and tightly trimmed. Should it transpire that the other yacht was larger, then "of course it will go faster than we do, it has a bigger LoA". If the yacht was

An early Start Line

smaller then "of course it will go faster than we do, it weighs less".

Rules were never used to win races, protests were seldom heard, and the Club's own special handicapping system, developed over the years since 1962 from Portsmouth Yardstick, Liverpool Bay rules and a general understanding that Boat A OUGHT to be able to beat Boat B, served well until the 1980's. It was generally accepted that engines would only be used if essential and that a short burst of power to avoid a channel buoy was not a worthy cause for disqualification. As explained in the adjoining excerpt from *the Venturer*, Venturers were not supposed to take racing **too** seriously.

Perhaps it was because John Partington (a keen racing man) became Vice commodore; perhaps it was because one or two quicker boats joined the Club; maybe it was because a Club boat merely had to be in the same stretch of water as the racers to be counted as a starter (even if it was wearing its ensign), but by 1985 over 20 boats were being reported as taking part in most of the races.

John also developed a fairer (he claimed) handicapping system which became known as the Club TCF (Time Correction Factor). Using this the total time was mathematically reduced and the smallest 'corrected time' was the winner. Points for winning were based on the usual principle of giving each boat the same number of points as their finishing position. So 5th (on handicap) would get 5 points: minimum number of points at the end of the season would win the overall race trophy - the Points Trophy. In the early days of the Club, the winner was awarded a maximum number of points. Thus six boats in a race meant that the winner gained 6 points - causing all sorts

Many cruising members worry about racing and why they don't do very well. The following notes may explain (or even help).

A standard rating certificate costs £2 but these are of little practical use. A better certificate can sometimes be obtained by negotiation - Flag Officers get these ex officio.

Rule 55b: no ordinary member shall approach the finishing line until all the Flag officers present have crossed it, and anchored (infringement of this rule leads to a variable penalty not disqualification - you would spot that).

Rule 57d: no boat shall start its engine within hearing of any other boat unless by mutual agreement, and then both boats shall do so.

Rule 58d: all engines must be stopped at least 5 cables from the finish (or half the total distance for courses of less than 5 cables).

of problems at the end of the season! At some point in time the practice of giving the winner an additional advantage by awarding a mere ½ point was abandoned and the RYA scheme was adopted.

The arrival of microcomputers helped.

Changes to the racing calendar came slowly because it seemed that a majority of Venturers enjoyed the "friendly" element as much as, if not more than, the "competitive" element of a race. Occasionally somebody would submit a Protest, but the general result was an admonition of the protestor for being a bad sport! As one Alan Hollingworth put it -"*It really about sail handling in close quarters*"

Start lines moved from the Clubhouse flagstaff, to the Royal Dee line at Trwyn Du (long since deceased), to Jack Orrell's house near Lleiniog Bay, to the Royal Anglesey line on Beaumaris Green. On balance Start lines some distance from the moorings increased the number of boats which arrived late - or under engine. The latter was seen as beneficial by some who carried way across the line.

RACING TROPHIES

	IN 1987	IN 2011
James Berry	To Moelfre. First race of the season	To Lynas Point
Irene Goodwin	To Moelfre. Ladies must helm.	To Conwy/Moelfre. Crew must helm.
Seamint	9 hour Race (used to be 8 hr race)	Passage race to Isle of Man
Astrador Cup	Puffin (Royal Dee line) to Holyhead	Puffin (defunct Royal Dee line) to Holyhead
Walton Shield	Holyhead to Caernarfon Bar	Holyhead to Caernarfon Bar
Firth	"Round the Cans". Last race.	Regatta "Round the Cans"
Trilogy		Time trial: select course and start time to gain best benefit from tides.
Whispered Secret		First Club yacht to finish the Menai Strait Regatta's Round Island race
Sprint		Regatta "Round the Cans"
Points	Series winner of all races	Series winner of all races

*Building the Lounge
between 1982 and 1986*

The Club ashore

While members were enjoying their sport afloat, there was a lot of activity around the Point and in particular within the Clubhouse. With membership never decreasing (even temporarily) the clamour for more space in the clubhouse grew. Crushing 50 to 100 people into the Galley/dining space for winter talks threatened to influence both audience and speakers against coming again. The 1980 Winter Programme listed an event every week.

In 1982 working parties involving no fewer than 40 members dug the foundations for a new Lounge. The Club's hopes for a substantial Sports Council grant were dashed when it was refused on the grounds that we had already started the work! It was 1984 before the Club could afford to erect walls and 1985 before the internal walls could be completed and the room connected to the existing building. At the same time the Changing Rooms block was in trouble. If current Health & Safety regulations had been in place they would have been closed as there was a real risk that somebody sitting down too heavily on the toilet could have fallen though, taking the WC with them!

It was mid-1987 before the Clubhouse would be declared 'fully fit for habitation' and by 1989 a further refurbishment of the Heads was under discussion.

The Club was also under pressure from other building schemes. The Royal Anglesey Yacht Club leased land alongside the Clubhouse and were talking about building new premises there: ABC were considered as leaseholders for the entire Point and, in 1986, the Nature Conservancy Council (NCC) laid claim to everything within yards of the HW line, from Trwyn Du (and beyond) to Caernarfon Bar. They seemed to be particularly determined to prevent spear-fishing for star fish in the Swellies. This was the first of a number of bids by conservationists to take control over the Club's sailing waters. The bid was fought off by the councils and all those with an interest in preserving the Menai Strait in its natural condition.

Administratively the Club made some momentous changes - motor cruisers were to be allowed into the Club! No more than 5%; and only if the owner had been a Club member and had swallowed the anchor. The Club continued to lease moorings from the council, ably re-distributed to Club members by Tony Stromberg, Moorings Officer for many years.

In 1988 membership records were transferred to a database (on a Personal Computer) with only two protestors. The database has developed over the years and provides the basis for communicating with members. It has now reached the stage where it is maintained on the Internet with options to pay subscriptions online.

25th Anniversary party

In 1986, the Club was 25 years old and held its Jubilee celebrations. Unfortunately these were very muted. A grand Jubilee race to the Isle of Man had to be cancelled because of gales. A grand Jubilee party in the Clubhouse suffered because the Lounge was still at foundation stage.

But the thought was there!

It was also in the Jubilee Year that the Club started to promote "Cruising Anglesey".

First Edition 1986
- Jubilee Year

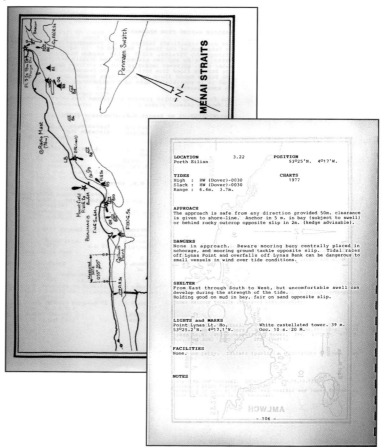

Anglesey Pilot

In the Golden Jubilee Year, "Cruising Anglesey" will have been around for 25 years.

Arthur Birtwistle and George Driver had created "Pilotage Notes" for half of Anglesey in 1978 leaving Ken Unsworth to complete notes for the rest of the Island. That was in addition to being Hon. Secretary and writing the Venturer each month. Hence in 1983 Ralph Morris volunteered to undertake the task.

As research into Part 3 got underway, it became clear that the definitive guide to the local waters, Henry Glazebrook's "Anglesey and North Wales Coast Pilot" was disappearing. A second edition of his work had been published by Yachting Monthly about the time the NWVYC was being formed but it was now out of print. When approached, YM indicated that not only did they have no intention of reprinting the guide, but would encourage and support a replacement pilot, incorporating Glazebrook's material.

Thus what had started as a completion of the Club's Pilotage Notes became an entirely new project - a rework of "Anglesey and North Wales Coast Pilot", with the blessing of Yachting Monthly, Glazebrook's publishers.

Norman Sheldrick, couldn't have put it better when he said, in his preface to the Yachting Monthly edition:

> Henry Glazebrook sailed coastwise from Trearddur Bay for many years in his 14ft dinghy 'Mermaid', and produced a book of sailing directions for the West coast of Anglesey under the title The Inshore Passage. This little book has long been out of print.
>
> For more than ten years Henry Glazebrook worked on a larger volume to cover the whole of the island coast as well as the coast of the mainland from the Point of Ayr right round to Portmadoc, drawing and redrawing the charts with all the current information available. This present book is the result of his meticulous work. While most of the sailing directions are applicable to all craft, it should be borne in mind that some of the inshore passage routes are suitable for dinghies only.

By November 1985 "Cruising Anglesey" was completed and, at a meeting during the Club's Dinner/Dance at the Queen Hotel in Chester, four Club members - John Powell, John Bennett, Ralph Hill and Ralph Morris financed its printing. The first 250 copies were sold before Christmas and in the New Year the Club started to advertise the reprint.

It was, at that time, an unashamedly amateur production: typed on a PC using graphics traced on the kitchen wall, it nevertheless still appeared to meet a need. By the end of the eighties, a second edition run of 1000 copies was on the shelves of most of the north west's chandleries.

Stock was held in the attics of the "Gang of Four", deliveries to chandleries were made in the back of their cars and Ralph Morris learned accountancy!

Another edition of 1000 copies followed in 1992 - updated from Notices to Mariners and a stream of typos fed back through the chandlers! A PBO reviewer complained that it did not include details of the whole of Cardigan Bay.

As the years passed, individual Club members joined forces with the author to market, distribute and manage growing sales. Over a 20 year period Godfrey Wilkinson distributed copies through his business in Sheffield, Brian Finney bulldogged recalcitrant chandlers, Des Booth chased advertisers and Ken Coles travelled the length and breadth of North Wales making sure that shelves were filled - not all at the same time.

Coverage expanded from only Anglesey to the entire coast from Liverpool to Porthmadog. The pilot was progressively renamed as the range increased until it stabilised on "Cruising Anglesey and adjoining waters".

Printing the cover in colour in 1999 generated a huge increase in sales and when Imrays took over publication in 2003 nearly 10,000 copies had been sold.

The initial financiers had been determined that the proceeds should go to the Club and by the time Imrays relieved individual Club members of the administrative load (and the Seventh edition), the Club had benefitted to the extent of some £40,000.

By 2010 Desktop Publishing software allowed the production of a full colour version on the Morris PC. Formally the pilot no longer has any connection to the Club, but due to the goodwill of Imrays and the original intent of the backers, the pilot still carries the Club logo and advertising revenue goes directly to the Club. It is the only Imray publication which carries advertising.

PUBLICATION HISTORY

1985	1st Ed	**"Cruising Anglesey"** with Glazebrook as a separate section.
1986		*Corrected & Reprinted twice*
1987		*Corrected & Reprinted*
1989	2nd Ed	**"Cruising Anglesey & North Wales"**. *Extended to Pt of Ayr and Pwllheli*
1991		*Corrected & Reprinted*
1992	3rd Ed	**"Cruising Anglesey & the North Wales Coast"**
1993	4th Ed	*Major update incl. withdrawal of RDF beacons*
1995	5th Ed	*Updated with new anchorages. Graphics digitised.*
1996		*Reprinted*
1998		*Corrected & Reprinted*
1999	6th Ed	**"Cruising Anglesey & adjoining waters"**. *Major rewrite. Extended to Liverpool, Glazebrook's pilot incorporated into pilot. Covers in colour. Indexed.*
2001		*Corrected & Reprinted*
2003	7th Ed	*Published by Imray. Chart Datum converted to WGS84*
2005		*Corrected & Reprinted*
2008		*Reprinted*
2010	8th Ed	*Extended to Porthmadog. Full colour with photographs & Google Earth inserts. First new cover photo since first edition. Printed & published by Imray.*

- *Seamint*
- *Aquayla drying the clothes in Scotland*
- *Club boats waiting for the tide*
- *Fiddler of Orwell at Abermenai*
- *Sheila Jones tends a Club BBQ*
- *Yet another Club social!*
- *GK heading for Tobermory*

Photos: John Partington & Vyv Cox

The Nineties

At last, after thirty years of growth (in every sense) the Club started to stabilise. The Programme had settled into a pattern, even to the extent that the Abermenai BBQ always happened in May and again in September. The Clubhouse had its Lounge and the Yearbook had an established content and style. The pilot was pulling in a consistent revenue (even after tax). The Club would have been able to relax - if it hadn't been for the influence of minority groups.

In 1987, the Nature Conservancy Council (NCC) had proposed that the whole of the Menai Strait, should become a Marine Nature Reserve (MNR), apparently if one read their documentation, as a means of preserving teaching and research specimens on the foreshore. The MNR was also intended to protect starfish (in the Swellies) from the depredations of spear-fishermen! The proposition was, of course, vigorously opposed by all Strait users and lovers. Various delays, including the NCC local man injuring himself in a sailing accident, meant that the "Strait Preservation Society" did not need to take any further action until 1993 when the document was re-issued by the Countryside Council for Wales (CCW) - the quango into which the NCC had morphed. By this time EU directives had given environmental groups a great deal of power and Wales was seen to be a soft option for introducing marine reserves in order to meet the UK's quota. Against that background, local opposition from most of North Wales forced a Public Meeting. The Inspector found against the CCW.

Things went quiet, and this appeared to be the end of the matter because nothing more was heard of the CCW - until Beaumaris Marina was mooted in 1998.

Moorings & Marinas

Well over a decade earlier, Dickies had proposed a marina in Hirael Bay. Generally welcomed it had been blocked by objections from a minority group of Welsh activists. In 1990 a marina development at Conwy almost met the same fate, whilst a development in Holyhead did. Club members hunkered down, avoided the politics in favour of enjoying sailing and faced a future of bouncing out to their moorings, protecting their belongings in black bin bags. Then in 1994 talk turned to marinas again; in Holyhead (again), Menai Bridge (or Beaumaris (Gallows Point)) and Victoria Dock (Caernarfon).

Each proposed marina was met with mixed feelings by Club members: though it is probably fair to say that those Club members who were most vociferous in their declared preference for getting their bottoms wet in dinghies were the ones who started to plan advance bookings for berths in the marinas. However, it wasn't till 1998 that formal proposals for a marina at Gallows Point were published. With support from Beaumaris town council as well as the county council it seemed that all would be well. Naturally the CCW objected.

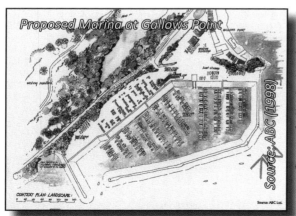

Proposed Marina at Gallows Point

Source: ABC (1998)

In 2004, after a Public Enquiry, the marina actually got a go-ahead. However Sue Ellis (AM) used her ministerial powers to have the project referred to the Welsh Assembly. (Before being elected, Sue Ellis had been deeply involved with ... the CCW.) **Back to the courts!**

At this point the CCW seemed to lose interest apparently relying on the Welsh Assembly to complete their work. However, unexpectedly, the Assembly members appointed to review the development, agreed it should go ahead, helped by some heavyweight legal persuasion. It was then that the mussel fishermen extended their objections to moorings to include marinas ....

In an entirely separate dispute, local mussel fishermen had resurrected a defunct fishing licence (the Menai Strait Oyster and Mussel Fishery Order 1962) for the waters between Beaumaris and the Gazelle. The mussel fishermen claimed Rights to all the seabed and demanded the removal of moorings. Entirely coincidentally, Club moorings began to disappear from the same stretch of seabed. Legal action was initiated against the mussel dredging operation and in addition to the councils and sailing clubs, the WYA, RYA and CCW (now an ally!) became involved.

It soon became clear that all the moorings north east of the Gazelle were at risk. It became equally clear that if the fishermen held the Rights to the seabed, then the council didn't. If the council didn't hold the Rights, then they would have been charging mooring fees illegally for twenty years!

In 1998 all moorings were removed from the waters between Gallows Point and the Gazelle - where the Club had started! But nobody got their money back.

The rest of the story properly belongs in the new millennium as CCW, fisheries and council (now joined by the Crown Commissioners), took it in turns to chase each other though the country's legal system. In the first *Venturer* of 2000, editor Ian Rodger announced "It now seems fairly certain that the marina ... will go ahead". Over the next few years he must have congratulated himself many times for including the word "fairly" . His successor wrote the same words in 2004 - as did his successor in 2008.

As the Club enters its fiftieth year, the paper chase continues, with the future of the Gallows Point marina, as well as that of Club moorings, hanging on the outcome of High Court, Welsh Assembly and perhaps even European, hearings.

Clubhouse development

In 1994 the Club won an award from the Foundation for Sport and the Arts to refurbish the existing Clubhouse, allowing the Heads rebuild (first seen to be essential in 1989) to go ahead. A comprehensive review of the state of the building produced a Wish List of compelling proportions and it was clear that the grant needed serious supplementary money to carry out all the work.

A short-list was compiled, comprising cladding the existing building, some shoring up of the foundations and a new foyer to form a staging area between the weather and the refurbished Galley/dining area. By 1998 the Clubhouse was declared 'finished'. Though

David Swinton at 40th Anniversary party

the Wish List was only half fulfilled, the remaining work was deferred until a resolution was found to the marina & moorings issues. The intention was to build a new Clubhouse within 10 years.

Venturing

Undeterred, members continued to *venture*. In 1995 Brian & Wendy Sharrock returned from their circumnavigation having brightened the decade's newsletters with regular stories of their adventures. Several other wanderers paid their subscriptions but were never seen at Gallows Point, being in the Med, the Caribbean, the Azores or merely France.

'Trumpeter' at the Fleet Review
Photo: Franco Lazoi

Ralph Hill, one of the pilot's original backers, made an eventful circumnavigation of the UK in aid of cancer research. He continues to defy doctors' predictions and published his memoirs "Salty Stories from the Chair" in 2009.

Closer to home, members turned up in numbers to join the Royal Yacht Britannia reviewing the fleet as part of the Battle of the Atlantic celebrations (1993). The fleet was expected to anchor in Table Roads between Moelfre and Traeth Coch. It blew easterly 8 - 10.

Several warships had to abandon their anchors and chain and retire to the River Mersey. Some decided that remaining on a secure anchorage at Menai Bridge was the prudent option and failed to make it to the Review.

Club members, not entirely believing the forecast of "Easterly gale 8 increasing severe gale 9" had turned up at the Club the previous evening with the intention of sleeping aboard and getting an early start the following morning. Other members turning up in the early morning found every inch of floor space occupied by a comatose body.

Alan Booth on *Trumpeter* (a Contessa 32) was the only Club boat to go out. Franco Lazoi, one of Alan's crew for the day, told it as he saw it, in yet another *Venturer* article .....

However I, perhaps slightly madder than most, had a quick breakfast, made some sandwiches, packed the sail bags, and set off for Beaumaris. At Gallows Point our skipper, Alan Booth, was waiting, hands in pockets and looking serious. Duncan, the junior crew member, was wearing a track in the beach, chewing gum and looking decidedly uncertain. Trevor, erstwhile fourth crew member, displayed none of this indecision. One quick glimpse of the lowering sky, an ear for the wind screaming through the rigging of the yachts still on land and he was off home to watch the Fleet review on the evening news from the comfort of his armchair. Other Club members had come down the previous night with the intention of sleeping on board. They were laid out in neat rows on the Clubhouse floor, exhausted and inclined to use the local pub's TV set to watch what promised to be a most interesting day.

It was almost low water, so we carried the inflatable and outboard down the beach and around the Point into the minimal shelter to the south west. After a few attempts we managed to scramble away towards Trumpeter, which was moored between Gallows Point and the Gazelle. By the time we reached her, we were soaked to the skin with waves breaking over the stem of the dinghy. Getting aboard was a tricky job and the first thing we did was change into dry clothing, have a cup of coffee and tie three reefs into the main. We motored against the wind, but with tide and made good progress to Puffin Sound, where we let out a scrap of roller reefing jib and set off at great speed towards the fleet which we could see in the distance. By this time we had both wind and tide with us and were making comfortable progress. We were very pleased with our decision to sail and could not understand why nobody else had made the effort to come along.

We set course towards Lynas, with the intention of passing outshore of the outer line, then turning to pass astern to review the second row. We were halfway through the first line of ships, which I was observing through binoculars, when Duncan, who was on the tiller, asked if I could take over as he was getting tired. I was rather surprised, as Duncan was a rugby player and by far the strongest of the three of us.

I could not believe how hard it was to control Trumpeter and keep her on course. I had to hold the tiller with both hands and put the whole weight of my body against it. I turned my head into the wind, which was by then blowing really hard, some gusts reportedly reaching 70 knots. The sea looked really nasty, steep, very steep, brown waves - not very high, perhaps, 2 metres, but very short. And it got worse as the tide turned. We struggled on deck and doused the mainsail as Trumpeter pitched high, coming clear of the water as far aft as the keel, then diving down into the troughs with a mighty crash.

The mast and rigging were vibrating so fiercely that we thought the mast might snap. The bow was going deep into each wave, with water flooding back into the cockpit and half filling it. Other times she would fall off into an empty space and my stomach came up into my mouth.

We decided to turn back. But how? To do so we had to be beam on to those increasing walls of water. I kept looking for a smaller wave and, when I saw one, I made a hard turn to port. Even this `small' wave caught us on the beam and we broached. It was sheer hell! Luckily we were all strapped in with double harnesses or we would have gone overboard. The force of the water pushed me against the pushpit, I lost the tiller and a 25 litre can of diesel was crushed. The mast touched the water and, as the boat righted herself, we found a cockpit filled knee high with a mixture of water and diesel. Not a good drink, and not a very effective eyebath! Fortunately the engine kept going and helped Trumpeter to complete the turn. We were able to shape a course for Puffin Sound, under the watchful eye of two coastguard cutters. We heard them on the radio saying "Keep an eye on that red yacht ..."

Motoring towards Puffin and the relative safety of the Menai Strait, I could see the sailors in full parade uniform on all those international ships, waving and clapping at us. I shall never know what they must have thought- stupid? - brave? - foolish? - or just plain crazy!

The 'Get Afloat' initiative

Maintaining and extending its training role, the Club had also introduced a 'Get Afloat' event offering a 'taster' of real sailing to people who did not have boats of their own and who had successfully completed an RYA shore-based course. In 1992 twenty nine boats replete with 'Get Afloaters' - or VICTIMS as they became known - cruised to the new Conwy marina. It was a total success with 134 sausages and 42 beefburgers devoured on the marina's new BBQ.

Forty two boats visited Conwy the following year to be entertained by Conwy Yacht Club. Used to seeing no more than three or four, the ladies of CYC, who could only see masts passing down the channel, prayed that every Venturer boat was a ketch. Victims came aboard on Sunday morning for the sail back to Beaumaris.

By 1994 it was obvious that the Conwy trip was to become a regular highlight of the cruising calendar. Then we went to Conwy again.

The Great Conwy Gale

John Powell of 'Tantaliza' tells this story:

The NWVYC fleet duly arrived at Conway Marina, to collect our respective "victims" who had been allocated to our boats for a sail back in company to Beaumaris.

Tantaliza's "Victims" included a young, but (let us kindly say) robustly constructed occasional dinghy sailor, and a very fit ex-soldier who had crewed on an army racing yacht and who, having been in the army, knew all about fore-decks and nothing else.

The forecast contained the possibility of SW force 6. But are we men or mice? And if our "victims" were to be given some REAL experience, better force 6 than a flat calm.

We sailed out of Conway alongside Mike Higgins' new motor-sailor (Mike changed his boats annually). Looking through my old photos there seems to have been good reason to suspect that "something was up", given the gallant way Mike's boat was already "Breasting the lofty surge" (Shakespeare).

We had Number 1 jib and full main.

Half way across to Puffin, it hit us suddenly and hard – with the crew not yet life-harnessed or other appropriate precautions taken. The "robust", but somewhat "ham-fisted" crew member managed to tumble headlong across the cockpit into a foaming lee rail. We heaved him back up and got everyone into life harnesses after which I got in a deep reef and the military man did his foredeck thing, setting the number 2 jib. Now under better control we rounded Puffin, and came hard on the wind, clawing up towards the Anglesey shore. Before us we witnessed a cluster of club boats anchored in the small bay just West of the light house. Tacking round behind them we established that they were not planning on going anywhere any time soon.

What to do? Well, what's wrong with the old adage, "go and have a look"? But first, a precaution: the final and deepest reef. We lay a-hull, thinking to stay under the cliffs during this exercise. Suddenly as I was about to sheet in, I heard a THUMP and was horrified to see the Dinmor buoy scraping down Tantaliza's side. Fortunately we were so pressed that the only thing that touched was the rubbing strip, which lived up to its name. More disconcerting was the sight of the loose arc of the topping lift just NOT lassoing the top of the buoy. In the time it took to take in a reef we had drifted one third of a mile.

Suitably humbled, we reached through Puffin Sound and started short-tacking up the straits. You know when it is really blowing, when weather bow wave turns into a continuous fire hose, pointed straight into your face. All was going well until the hanks started pulling out of the jib luff. We dropped it, started the 10 HP Bukh, and carried on, taking wide "motor-tacks", to keep way on, passing the Beaumaris moorings (which did not look habitable) and picking up a buoy near to Menai Bridge. Damage consisted of the No. 2 jib, a burst dodger, and lot of water in the most unlikely places. My "victims" had had a great time and wanted to do it all over again.

The autopsy on the event produced the following: Only two boats got back to the moorings – Tantaliza and Whispered Secret. The rest stayed on at their various anchorages or returned to Conway, except Conachair, who went to Moelfre, and where their "victims" paid a fishing boat £5 each to take them off. One small "family" cruiser – rather flat bottomed, bilge keels etc - could only make ground to windward to round Puffin by using sail and engine, at which point the engine cut out and she had to be rescued by the life boat. People with those whirly things that tell you how windy it is so you know when to be frightened, reported gusts of over 50 knots. (We do not have a whirly thing). It does leave you with the thought that, when the chips are down, there is no substitute for windward capability. Maybe that's why we still have the same boat.

That day, Moelfre and Beaumaris lifeboats answered calls from 15 boats in difficulties in the Strait between Conwy Fairway Buoy and Puffin Island. Others, as John Powell saw, sheltered to the north of Trwyn Du. In the final wash up, the general consensus was that it is better to gain your experience of heavy weather in the straits than twenty miles offshore.

There were no more 'Get Afloat' events. Somebody also mentioned that the Club might need to take out insurance in case a Victim sued!

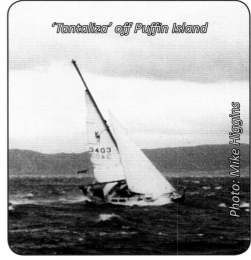

'Tantaliza' off Puffin Island

Photo: Mike Higgins

The era in which no good deed goes unpunished was truly arriving at the NWVYC.

Political correctness affected power supplies from the clubhouse to club boats wintering on Gallows Point, refurbishment of the clubhouse, Winter events and even the laying of moorings. And it spelled the end of TBT antifouling - though it was a few years before individual's stockpiles were fully exhausted.

Still, the Rock Trophy continued to be passed from skipper to skipper, every one of them honouring John Powell by creating a tradition of always accompanying the knowing smile with a poem. Nobody surpassed Linda Moss (in 1998) when she shopped her skipper (husband Scott Moss) by writing a poem for the existing holder to present to him. Mind you, he did put 'Conachair' aground outside the Clubhouse window!

Conachair at Bardsey Island

PHOTO: Vyv Cox

Linda was later to become the Club's second female commodore, the honour for being the first going to Sandra Finney in 1997.

We had entered the decade with 150 boats in the club; we left it with 135 boats and some 250 members. Interestingly Club numbers peaked in 1995 at 298 members (153 boats) and reached their lowest level in 20 years just three years later (219 members with 130 boats).

The end of the millennium also saw the end of another era - RDF beacons were switched off and in sympathy we had a total eclipse of the Sun.

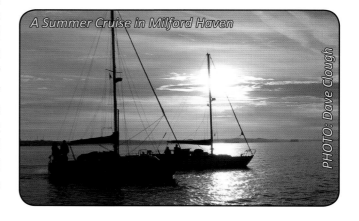

A Summer Cruise in Milford Haven

PHOTO: Dave Clough

The New Millennium

"2000 started in fine style with the Millennium party, preceded by our own Millennium Beacon, lit at 1910hrs as part of the National chain". And that's how commodore Linda Moss reported the start of the 21st century in *the Venturer*.

The upbeat theme continued as, in March, Beaumaris Marina was given the OK (yet again) and the Club launched a survey to establish how its members thought it should capitalise on the opportunities the marina and newly announced Objective 1 funding might bring.

- *Do we want to maintain the DIY character of the Club?*
- *Do we want to retain the Clubhouse or consider moving into the marina?*
- *Do we want to extend our range of activities?*
- *Do we want to encourage marina-based members?*

'Yes', 'Stay', 'Don't know', 'Good question' were the answers.

We rescued 'Harry Furlong' buoy on the north coast of Anglesey from Trinity House cutbacks.

There were a few minor problems:

- *CCW refused to accept defeat and forced a Public Enquiry into the marina*
- *A major outbreak of Foot & Mouth disease virtually quarantined Anglesey*
- *GMDSS was introduced with, of particular interest (or concern) to yachtsmen, DSC (Digital Selective Calling).*

After the problems of the late 1990s, the Club had no difficulty taking all the problems in its stride -and maintaining a suitable irreverent sense of humour, as John Lomas's Y2K Log (see over) demonstrated.

Sailing throughout the decade, with a few notable exceptions such as Gerry Lomax who took 'Nell Gwyn' across the Atlantic, centred around the Irish Sea. The long hauls to the outermost reaches of Scotland diminished as exploration of the Welsh and Irish coasts prevailed. Many Summer Cruises explored the secret anchorages, and Bars, of Cardigan Bay, but it took "Cruising Anglesey "

Continued on page 46

Day 1, 05.00 hrs. Sailed off mooring. Verbally abused by youths on shore in Friars Bay (they could have been shouting for help, I suppose). Responded in manner they clearly understood. Overtaken by yacht Menai One motoring. Smelt bacon. Crew's request to share breakfast politely refused. Pleased to hear later that smug youth on helm of Menai One spent the day being seasick. Enough petrol on board to motor to IoM and back twice. Smell of petrol and bacon adds to my growing queasiness. (We can only smell petrol when boat is heeled and/or pitches. It does both for much of next few days). Cheerful response from Holyhead Coastguard when I report our intentions.

05.35 Sea beyond Puffin Sound sighted. The words "Cape" and "Horn" spring to mind. Dinghy hastily hauled on board. Sails reefed. Breakables stowed. Another Kwell taken.

06.00 First wave breaks over bow, shortly followed by one of its many friends who break over the boat. Dinghy partially washed overboard. Crew wet. I have serious thoughts of other places to go rather than PSM (like home). Water in left wellie resurrects trench foot from dinghy sailing days.

06.10 Unaccountably large amount of water below. First of many bucketful's removed. Major source of problem identified. Hair-raising trip to anchor locker to close mushroom vent. Locker full of water and mostly draining into boat, not out. (When telling this tale to a couple from Liverpool the following day, they knew someone who made an identical mistake but had their hatch cover over and washboards in. By the time they discovered the problem, their dog was swimming around the cabin)

06.15 Following serious debate we settle down to a wet fetch in a confused sea. (I am equally confused as to why we do these things.) Discover vent still leaks slightly and that weight forward when bailing makes the problem worse as bow buries even more. Decide to bail only when sufficient depth of water to bail from well back. Spare battery wet and giving off noxious gas. Wet GPS claims we are doing 22 knots and our course is the opposite of the one we are on. It wants to go home too. Bright sunshine and clear sky from above, F5/6 in left ear. Frequent breaking waves from sea on beam quickly re-wets anything the sun and wind dries. Remembering now why I gave up dinghy sailing, although the wet suit would be handy at the moment. I feel unwell and sleepy, probably due to time of morning, the odd can or so last night and 2 Kwells (see above). Coastguard snotty when I request an up-to-date weather forecast. Suggests we listen in on Ch 10 in 2 minutes time. Ouch! IoM sighted before noon.

12.30 Arrive PSM. Report arrival to Liverpool Coastguard as requested by Holyhead earlier in the day. Eventually tie up against inner harbour wall and return rest of Irish Sea to where it belongs. We make a passable illusion of competency even though I had never before moored alongside anything, ever. Menai One apparently arrives after us. Vent sealed with long piece of Elephant tape. Decline opportunity to enter following day's 'Round the Island Race'.

Day 2 Just when my head and stomach were threatening to return to normal, rash enough to go on the I.o.M. steam railway and an electric tram. Both these modes of transport make the passage over seem quite smooth by comparison. Settled by several pints of TT2000 bitter. Bay View Hotel is deservedly honoured by our patronage. Albert Hotel looks to be a hangout for ruffians as well as having one sign that says "food served every day" and another that says "no food served today". How far from Ireland are we? Hospitable yacht club full of crews who had just completed race (see above). First boat finished in just over 12 hours.

Day 3, 09.00 hrs. Weather forecast dictates a quicker than expected return (windy today, windier tomorrow, worse by the day after and "don't bother going home your house will have blown down" for the day after that). Had planned to go to Strangford Loch but that is the direction the wind is coming from. Inform Liverpool of intentions. Dead run, reach and close reach as the wind moves from NW to W and eventually SW.

Crew dislikes downwind sailing in prevailing conditions and becomes abusive when I suggest spinnaker. We sailed 505s together once and he knows what usually happens when I put up the "death cloth". Stroke of navigational genius makes us set course for Holyhead knowing the tide will push us along the coast to Cemaes in one long "ferry glide". Anchored at Lamb Island by 18.00. 9 hours from PSM. Try to inform both Liverpool and Holyhead Coastguard of arrival. No response from either although can clearly hear other traffic. In pub by 19.30 watching children struggle with the unfamiliar concept of using a knife and fork, sitting still and keeping their mouths shut long enough to keep the food in. All establishments that serve food should be made to create booths and erect screens so that the dire table manners of some can be hidden from public view. Left as pathetic youth of 12/13 was having his meat cut up for him by his mother, a task he appeared to be incapable of himself. Crew and I list all our pet hates over a tumbler or two of whiskey back on board. I am high on his list (snoring, chronic intolerance, etc). Most of humanity qualify for mine. Crew says I only sail because pavement cyclists and dog walkers are not usually found at sea. Point out fishermen and motor boats are adequate substitutes. Crew regards my views on a punitive tax on dogs, cycles and PWCs as extreme. I feel duly complimented. Manage to raise Holyhead but my message to them is not clearly received. Work out Lamb Island is not a good reception area. Probably the fault of the power station. Later caught 3 eyed fish from a glowing green sea.

Day 4 Catch last of morning flood to Bull Bay. Pick up mooring off village who says "we should pull in a bit of chain on a 27ft tide". Don't understand what he means, so don't. Walk to Amlwch. Sunbathe outside hotel in Bull Bay. Return to Silver Apple to find rocks have appeared less than 2 metres from stern. Finally understand advice of mooring owner (see above) and why anchorage is marked on chart as being elsewhere in bay. Round Point Lynas on late afternoon flood (saw dolphin- not the yacht- the swimming mammal/ fish/ stops your manic depression/cures your ills if you swim with it/ etc.). Seals aplenty on Ynys Dulas. Tie up at Moelfre for the night. Crew announces pub has no atmosphere, food is overpriced and is the worst of the trip so far. Gets no argument from me. At least it's so unpopular we're spared the spectacle of slurpers, gobblers, pickers, cement mixers, Italians, finger lickers and all the other variants of modern McDonalds / Simpsons style of eating.

Day 5, 06.00 hrs Early start to return to Beaumaris. Enjoyable reach to Puffin and a beat up the Straits under full sail in a good F3+. Sailed on to mooring at around 09.00. Why is no one ever watching when you get this right first time and everyone is watching when you don't? Still enough petrol on board to motor to the IoM and back twice!

Late lunch in the Gazelle where £3.78 for a pint of mild and a pint of bitter shandy is the late winner of the "rip off of the week" award. Runner up, Kinmel Arms. Star of the week, dead heat between Bay View (PSM) and Miner's Arms (Laxey).

Continued from page 43

until 2010 to catch up by extending coverage to Porthmadog.

Racing continued to be enthusiastically perpetrated - though questions about Starting Flag signals in the Social Quiz Nights produced uniformly blank faces (with the exception of the Club President who still managed the handicapping system).

Rock Trophy poems were regularly published in *the Venturer* which changed its editor in 2001. When Ian Rodger had accepted the role of Hon Secretary, the newsletter had come as part of the bundle; in fact the newsletter had always been a

Lamb Island anchorage, Cemaes Bay

PHOTO: Glen Warburton

millstone the Hon. Secretary had to carry. In the most part, they all revealed themselves as writers of quality; one could imagine that the job of 'Hon. Secretary' came as a millstone that aspiring newsletter editors had to face.

Twenty first century communications

Ian's management of *the Venturer*, turning it into a quality journal, had resulted in the committee asking him to continue when he relinquished the Secretary role. Thus, the two jobs became separated. When he felt it was time to retire, the position of Editor was formalised and became an *ex-officio* position on the Management Committee. After all, how else could he/she get all the inside gossip to spread to the membership. The role was taken over by Ralph Morris and coordinated with that of webmaster for the Club's newly developed web site:

www.nwvyc.org.uk

Six years later the dual role transferred to Carolyn Warburton who extended the number of cruising articles in the newsletter and, being a software professional, brought an altogether more professional approach to the website.

Throughout the decade, the triple thrust of newsletter, web site and email has substantially raised the level of communication between club members. This has been particularly marked in the last three years when Internet technology has enabled a degree of two way contact which had not been previously possible. Everything from planning cruises to advertising the Lifeboat Day is now just a bulk email away. The challenge for the current committee is to increase the flow of information without turning it into spam.

As a result of these advances in communications, the Club has been able to undertake more activities both afloat and ashore - and to change the Programme at much shorter notice than was possible in the days of snailmail. Winter talks (and suppers), Boat Jumbles and book sales (we have become agents for Imrays publications) all benefitted from better contact. As did sales of artefacts, general chandlery and Club merchandise.

There had always been a 'Bosun's Store', typically a broken cardboard box with Club burgees, ties and the occasional sweater - but never in the right size. Custodianship of the Store had rested haphazardly on the shoulders of the Rear commodore, who frequently did not find out about his duty until after his appointment. Some were natural salesmen and in their reigns most members sported Club sweaters at parties. But whoever was in charge, everybody had a burgee made in Hong Kong.

When Dave Clough volunteered for the job in 2006 he brought a much more positive (some said aggressive!) approach. Now members not only have sweaters but baseball hats, fleeces, rugby shirts and our own brand of cleaning materials for the boat. Members arriving at the Clubhouse with clothing which does not sport Ebb & Flo move furtively until they are assured that Dave is not around. Burgees now last more than a single season and are made in the UK. The Club has a new income stream! Then 'Google Checkout' arrived. Members can now order and pay for their regalia online. And all excuses for not paying subscriptions on time have been removed - for everybody with Internet access.

In 2010 the membership database was transferred online and on its fiftieth birthday the Club is as advanced in its communications with members as any in the country.

Other opportunities it did not grasp with the same level of enthusiasm. When the government announced the option of Community Sports Club status (CASC) in 2005 it was initially seen as a generous offer - less tax for every Sports Club which signed up. Closer inspection, however, showed that the contract forced clubs to accept some fairly fundamental political doctrines, a number of which were the antithesis of the Club's tenets.

In 2009 the Club finally shelved the option.

Gallows Point developments

Alongside the internal activities of the Club, ran the machinations surrounding the marina, the moorings and a Special Area of Conservation (SAC) which had somehow been slipped through 'under the radar' by CCW while everybody was arguing about the other issues. Attention had been diverted from the CCW's subterfuges by a grandiose development scheme sponsored by Anglesey County Council (2001) and then by a counter-bid by some local residents to have Gallows Point declared a "Village Green" (2005).

Complaints about the dilapidated, not to say dangerous, state of Gallows Point had been aired for more than the previous decade and the council had proposed action on several occasions. The first mention in Club records being in the mid-70s. The Millennium scheme, launched on the back of Objective 1 funding entailed three options. The "moderate intervention" option included a wooden promenade deck cantilevered over Beaumaris Bay between Gallows Point and the town. This was to be ideally placed to capture the full impact of easterly gales (sic!). In addition most of the buildings on Gallows Point were to be razed and ABC was to build new ones - to rent to the owners of the sheds ... which were to be razed! This did not sit well with the shed owners. In retribution they lodged a petition to declare Gallows Point a 'Village Green'. Yet another Public Enquiry ensued at which the petitioners presented no evidence. They had discovered that success would mean that their sheds would have to come down.

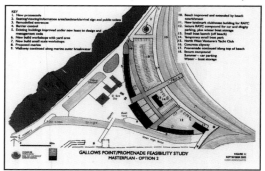

GALLOWS POINT/PROMENADE FEASIBILITY STUDY
MASTERPLAN - OPTION 2

Throughout all this, NWVYC was in the comfortable position that its premises were ring-fenced. Royal Anglesey YC, who leased a small plot next to the Club was to be given a prime site for a "new landmark clubhouse building" at the end of the Point adjacent to a walkway around the marina. ABC Power Marine, developers of the marina, were to be given management of the entire Point - except the RAYC and NWVYC sites. With the exception of making ABC the landlords almost all the other proposals were dependent on the marina.

In 2011 only the transfer of the Head Lease to ABC has taken place. The marina is still moot, the Point is not a Village Green and the moorings still may, or may not, be in the gift of the council; which doesn't stop the annual mooring fee demand dropping through members' letter boxes.

Onwards

Throughout the last ten years, navigation and Aids to Navigation have changed out of all recognition. Trinity House are steadily withdrawing buoys and lighthouses, the UKHO no longer promise to maintain the accuracy of charts for small ports and GPS is *de rigeur*. Chart plotters have flourished and yachts have multiplied the number of heavy duty batteries carried. It is a sad fact that an electrical failure can cripple many modern yachts and devastate their skippers.

Not a Venturer's yacht though! **WE** still carry charts, plan cruises on paper and generally do our best to uphold the traditions of good seamanship.

In 2008 the RYA renewed the Club's authority to grant RYA (shore-based) certificates and it is now a recognised RYA Training Centre presenting all the courses of benefit to a cruising sailor. Derek Lumb, who had been in many of the decade's initiatives, was the school's first principal. He relinquished the post to Ralph Morris in the anniversary year.

After fifty years of growth, the Club's essence is unchanged and unfaltering:

To encourage cruising in sailing boats and to study the principles of navigation and seamanship.

As a result, in many cases a direct result, of the Club's tenets, Ebb & Flo are seen around the World. One Club member, sailing in France, was recognised by a yacht which had recently returned from New Zealand. That yacht had met 'Helgi II' (Brian & Wendy Sharrock) carrying Ebb & Flo on her self-steering in Auckland, New Zealand.

Gallery

'Kate' races 'Winfarthing'!
PHOTO: David Clough

Typically Gallows Point

Clearing the prop – Venturers style
PHOTO: Derek Lumb

Menai Bridge

'Tiger Lily'
PHOTO: David Clough

Amlwch Port

Unattributed photos were taken by the author

Cable Bay anchorage
PHOTO: John Lomas

'Patsy' 1964

'Spartan Warrior'
PHOTO: Dave Clough

Summer cruise in Penzance
PHOTO: Dave Clough

Summer cruise in Portpatrick
PHOTO: Vyv Cox

'Good Knews' winning the Irene Goodwin Trophy
PHOTO: Vyv Cox

'Skibbereen'
PHOTO: Vyv Cox

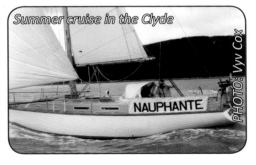
Summer cruise in the Clyde
NAUPHANTE
PHOTO: Vyv Cox

Antifouling Test

9723 T

SARICO

PHOTO: Joe Presford

The Great Conwy Gale

PHOTO: John Powell

Abermenai anchorage

Training Day with the RNLI & RAF Valley SAR

PHOTO: Glen Warburton

Summer cruise to Brittany

'Olimilo' out in front

PHOTO: Dave Clough

Pen-y-Parc anchorage

PHOTO: Derek Lumb

Trwyn Du

PHOTO: Dave Clough

Ebb & Flo off Bora Bora

PHOTO: Brian & Sandra Finney

Menai Strait from Puffin Island

PHOTO: Derek Lumb

'Osprey' at Llanddwyn

PHOTO: Lee Downs

Appendices

I - Presidents & Commodores

PRESIDENTS

1966-1983	Judge Meurig Evans
1995-1998	Arthur Birtwistle
1999-2004	Gordon Rutter
2005-	John Partington

COMMODORES

1962-1966	Judge Meurig Evans	*Maid of Menai*	1991-1993	Michael Higgins	*Royal Flush*
1967-1969	John Osola	*Osprey of Doune*	1994-1995	Ralph Morris	*Trilogy*
1970-1972	Christopher Hind	*Ewig Wen*	1996	Vyv Cox	*Straitshooter*
1973-1975	Bernard Hallé	*Timbatoo*	1997-1998	Sandra Finney	*Alanah of Gigha*
1976-1977	Christopher Buck	*Sinbad*	1999	Brian Parr	*Dolphin*
1978-1979	Arthur Birtwistle	*Minella*	2000-2001	Dr Linda Moss	*Conachair*
1979-1981	Dr John Bennett	*Avilion*	2002-2004	John Lomas	*Enigma*
1982-1984	Gordon Rutter	*Seamint*	2005-2007	Alan Hollingworth	*Chinook*
1985-1987	John Partington	*Gunsmoke*	2008-2009	Jean Lumb	*Whispered Secret*
1988-1990	Bernard Hobart	*Nauphante*	2010-	Paul Mountford	*Snowbird*

II - St Kilda Trophy

1975	*Lindora*	Dick Partington
1979	*Sinbad*	Chris Buck
	Minella	Arthur Birtwistle
1988	*Seamint*	Gordon & Marjorie Rutter
	Solitaire	Geoff & Vera Schofield
1990	*Junkette*	Ralph Hill
1993	*Tumbler*	Brian & Alma Butterworth with Hazel Hayes
1993	*Minella*	Mike & Sue Lyskey with John Harrison
1994	*Vida of Menai*	Roy Trick & Jenny Draper
1996	*Skibbereen*	Peter Thomas
1998	*Piper*	David Rainsbury
2000	*Piper*	David Rainsbury
2001	*Minella*	Roger Chisholm
2005	*Meganza*	Charles Townley

III - The Beginnings

At the beginning of the 1961 season, the NW Group of the Silhouette Owners Association had asked Storm Bate and Geoff Walton, who both lived in North Wales, if they would act as a Racing and Cruising Sub-Committee for the Group. They did much of the detailed planning for the Isle of Man cruise in 1961 from which the concept for the North West Venturers Yacht Club emerged.

In the following notes, they sum up the operation, and some of the lessons learned.

"We spent a great deal of time in preparing detailed plans covering such items as safety gear to be carried, methods of communication by day and night, and in devising code signals and code names for boats, the position each boat in the fleet, and the course to be followed, calculated upon an average speed of three knots. It was decided to lay a course going out for Langness Point, and that if there was to be any error it should be to the North West.

Before sailing, all skippers were briefed on the plans, and the latest met. reports. Anti-seasickness pills were available for those who wished. It had been decided originally that each boat should be checked for seaworthiness and safety gear, but in the rush of loading stores and preparing for sea there just was not time.

It had also been decided that a minimum crew of three should be on each boat as a precaution against seasickness and other contingencies which might leave a boat undermanned. In the end this rule had to be waived, for otherwise some could not officially have started, but would probably have come just the same.

By compass the course was as reasonably correct as one can maintain in a small boat, though initially the ebbing tide seemed to be setting the fleet slightly East. At 19.00 on the evening of the passage the wind was still Force 4 on the Ventimeter, and the fleet's speed was averaging five knots. Owing to the varying speeds of the various boats, it was found that it was too difficult for boats to keep station. Although a different line-up was used for the return journey, again it was found that (apart from three boats) the prescribed positions were not kept. Those in front found it inconvenient to heave to for the whole fleet to foregather properly before darkness fell, though an effort was made to slow down by letting the jibs fly.

As darkness came on the way over the fleet was scattered over an estimated two to three mile line. Every skipper had been advised that he must be prepared to act on his own, and each man was very much on his own. It was soon apparent that our speed was such that we were going to arrive some two or three hours before the ETA, and since it had been calculated that there would have been a full beam tide in both directions to cancel each other out, there would have been a corrected course advised to the fleet at about 01.00. The fleet, however, was too scattered for this to be done, and in the main it carried on, each skipper on his own, but following the set course.

The result was that the full flood set the fleet some eight miles East, and there was no tide for the ebb correction. Consequently the landfall was Douglas Head and not Langness.

Most of the fleet picked up the Douglas Head Light at about 03.00, but within a few minutes it had disappeared in the rain. Individually, the boats made for the only light they had seen, and at 04.00 most were standing around off Douglas waiting for daylight to show up the coast. Geoff Walton, however, in Two Gees, had altered course at 02.25, headed straight for Langness Point, and sailed into Carrick Bay. The main body of the fleet was identified by him about six miles to the East. The wind having fallen light, all boats put on their motor, and motorsailed into bay, except for Herbert Firth, whose motor, unknown to others, had broken down. The fleet was tied up by 8 am at Port St Mary, except Herbert Firth's Dolphin, who was trying to get in under sail alone against a foul tide, and did not berth until near 11.00. There was no danger to Dolphin, and had the skipper been anyone less than Herbert someone would have gone out and towed them in; since it was Herbert, the rest of the fleet were at a loss to understand what was holding him back. At the same time, to have gone out and towed in Dolphin would have been a kindness after such a trip.

Log of 1961 Isle of Man Cruise
By Geoff Walton

This is the log kept by Geoff Walton (G. J. Walton) of his passage in the Silhouette II 'Two Gees' from Glyn Garth in the Menai Straits to Port St Mary, Isle of Man, and back, in company with three other Silhouettes ('Dolphin', Herbert Firth, 'Buttercup II', R. Bradbury, and 'Kotka', Ian Holyman) two Caprices ('Sampan', Don McKnight and 'Sainfoin', James Berry) a Leeward ('Eileen', Storm Bate) and a Mystic ('Karena', Wilfred Jacques). The seven ton sloop 'Maid of Skye', (Judge Meurig Evans) sailed with the fleet. Geoff Walton sailed with his son, G. G. Walton, as crew.

July 29. 10.00. Fitted lifelines, made inventory of safety gear checked flares, etc. General check of boat and gear, fitted new locking wire on rigging screws and shackles.

21.00. Crews' meeting at the Gazelle. All members briefed, course checked, call signs (Morse flashes) and information plans distributed, safety precautions checked. All crews satisfied with arrangements.

July 30. 09.00. Obtained met. forecast from RAF, Valley. Wind WNW, Force 4. Informed all members that departure would be 16.15. Coastguards at Penmon, Point Lynas and Port St Mary informed.

11.30. Provisioned craft and made ready to drop moorings at Beaumaris.

15.00. Cast off, sailed to Glyn Garth and tied up to jetty.

16.15. Departed Glyn Garth and set course for Puffin Sound. Fleet looked very impressive. GG at helm.

17.20. Entered Puffin Sound.

17.25. Sound now clear. Set course 345°. Wind WSW, Force 3-4. Moderate beam sea. Speedometer reading 4.5 knots.

17.35. Passed Ten Foot Bank buoy on starboard. On course 345°

18.30. GJ at helm, dined on roast chicken and coffee. On course 345°. Plenty of visibility.

20.30. GG at helm, on course, but according to back bearings on Great Orme and Point Lynas appear to be making more leeway than estimated. Fortunate that it is an easterly drift. Will probably put us off

Douglas. Wind WSW, Force 4. 4.5 knots.

22.30. GJ at helm. On course 345°. Wind now W Force 4.

23.30. Glow from Douglas on horizon, confirms leeway. Unable to get satisfactory back bearings as Orme Light not working. Managed rough check on Lynas Light.

July 31. 00.30. GG at helm, on course 345°. Beautiful night, all fleet visible.

02.20. H. Firth fired white Verey light, large steamer seems rather close, but deceptive at night, probably well clear. GJ at helm On course 345°. Wind W. Force 4. Five knots. Should beat ETA if wind holds.

02.25. Heavy sea mist forming, with rain. Fleet now out of sight. Changed course to 305° This should keep us clear of coast. Wind W. Force 4-5, fairly heavy seas. Boat very dry.

03.05. Seemed to hear heavy engines. Shone torch on sails and had Verey pistol to hand. Not needed, probably imagination. Coffee and sandwiches.

04.00. GG at helm. On course 305°

04.18. Light on port quarter observed, timed flashes and identified Langness Rock.

04.25. Light to starboard, identified as Douglas Head. Held course 305°. Wind WNW, Force 5. Heavy seas.

04.30. Changed course to 260° to keep clear of Langness Race.

05.00. Maid of Skye observed to port, approx. three miles, on course for Port St Mary. Nasty sea running. Visibility now good.

06.00. Able to identify rest of fleet, approx. six miles astern in direction of Douglas.

06.05. GJ at helm. Decided to sail into Carrick Bay to take advantage of lee from high ground and wait for rest of fleet.

07.35. Arrived Port St Mary and tied up to wall astern of herring fleet. Very tired, but extremely pleased that voyage had turned out so well. Met by Secretary of IOM Yacht Club, who gave us the freedom of the club. Hot showers available, also food. Very nice gesture. Cleaned selves and boat and had large breakfast.

13.00. Moved to Inner Harbour, much better berth on sandy bottom. Wind NNW, Force 1-2, with sunshine. The party spent the next two days in the Isle of Man, enjoying the generous hospitality of the IOM Yacht Club and of other friends in the Island. The fleet set off to return on August 3.

August 3. 04.45. Cast off, and formed up in bay. Nasty red sky, with wind clouds forming. GG at helm.

05.00. On course 160°, wind light from West. Dull.

06.15. GJ took over. On course 160°. Wind W. Force 2. Barometer 29.75 falling.

07.00. Maid of Skye sailed over to inform us that the shipping forecast was giving SW, Force 6. Made immediate decision to turn back. Put about, and headed on visual course to Port St Mary.

08.00. GG at helm. Wind W. Force 3-4. Heavy rain and nasty swell.

08.10. Started engine to enable us to make harbour on one leg.

09.15. GJ at helm. Heavy rain, Wind WSW, Force 3-4.

09.50. Tied up to wall in Outer Harbour. Changed clothes, breakfast and sleep.

15.00. Moved under power to Inner Harbour. Heavy seas running, wind about Force 6, SW.

15.30. All boats tied up and snug, decision to return very wise. Wind now Force 8 from SW, with heavy rain.

August 4. Shipping forecast for 24 hours wind W. backing SW Force 5-6. Will listen to midnight forecast for further decision.

August 5. 00.02. Forecast SSW, Force 5-6. Back to bed.

10.00. Moved to Outer Harbour which does not dry out; wise precaution if we have to get away smartly. Provisioned.

14.00. Forecast, wind WSW, Force 4-6. Further decision later. Had short sail round bay to check conditions. Found that with this wind it would be just possible to hold our homeward course of 162°, but would certainly make a great deal of leeway. Conditions extremely uncomfortable.

17.58. Forecast, wind WSW, Force 4-5, gusting 6. Voyage postponed.

18.15. Phoned Ronaldsway, who gave a 12 hour forecast, wind W. Force 3-4. Seems like a good chance. Barometer rising steadily.

18.30. Skipper's meeting Decision made to leave at 01.00 tomorrow if 00.02 forecast is favourable.

August 6. 00.02. Forecast, wind WSW, Force 4-5, gusting 6. Back to bed.

13.40. Forecast, wind veering later NW, Force 4-6. Decided to meet again at 17.58. Looks as if it may be possible to leave this evening or early morning. Made boat ready for passage, and had a couple of hours sleep.

17.58. Forecast, wind WSW, Force 3-4. Decided to sail at 19.00. Course to be 200° until nightfall, and then 160° for second leg.

19.00. Cast off and formed up in bay. Large crowd of friends and well wishers on quay. Beautiful evening, with clear sky, sea slight. Wind WSW, Force 2. Barometer 30.26. GJ at helm.

19.25. Set course 200° started Seagull, as only two knots on speedometer. About one third throttle brought speed up to four knots.

20.30. GG at helm. Course 200°. Topped up fuel tank, rather awkward in swell. Wind WSW, Force 2. Making four knots. Visibility unlimited.

21.25. GJ at helm. Good back bearing on Chicken Rock and Langness. Dead on course.

22.30. Engine topped up. Lights on port bow, probably North Stack and Skerries, but too early yet for positive identification. Fantastic amount of phosphorescence in water, prop. leaving long wake of flame.

23.20. GG at helm. Back bearing good, changed course to 160°. Wind SW, Force 2, engine great help, making four knots.

23.59. On course 160° Hot soup and sandwiches.

August 7. 00.30. GJ at helm. Passed Maid of Skye to port.

01.00. On course 160°. Topped up engine.

02.20. Skerries and North Stack now positively identified. Altered course to 150° for Lynas. Would appear to be leading the fleet now, as we are getting replies to our lamp signals from astern.

03.00. Two large steamers crossed our bows, going E to W. approx. two miles ahead. Topped up engine.

03.45. GG at helm. On course 150°. Wind SW, Force 2. Easy sea. Coffee and chocolate. Further lights now identified as Point Lynas, Penmon, Orme and Moelfre. Also useful check on Amlwch ICI works lights. Sky now lightening in East.

04.30. Dawn, landfall made W of Point Lynas. Changed course to 140°, for Puffin Sound.

05.30. Trawler passed to starboard, steaming in N direction. On visual course for Puffin Sound all fleet now visible, approx. five miles astern.

Topped up engine, increased power, as wind now variable, Force 1.

05.45 GJ at helm.

06.30. On course for Puffin, beautiful morning, calm sea.

07.00. Topped up engine. GG at helm. Took off oilskins.

01.15. Entered Puffin Sound and signalled to Coastguard. Wind now Force 0. Sea like millpond.

08.20. Left Sound, dropped sails and stowed gear. Tide just right, approx. HW slack. Topped up engine.

08.45. Picked up mooring at Beaumaris. Loaded gear in dinghy and tidied ship. Ashore in time to see fleet pass up the Straits for Glyn Garth.

IV - Junior Log Winner 1963

THE CRUISE OF THE LEEWARD SLOOP *EILEEN*

An account of the Whitsun cruise based on the log of Eileen a 19ftx14ft9inx7ft Leeward Bilge Keel Sloop by Storm Bate.

The Met Office at Valley on Saturday, 9th June, 1962, forecast winds south west going to North West, wind speed, not more than 10 knots,.

Over the condemned man's lunch at the Gazelle Hotel, Wilf Jacques, Skipper of the Mystic Class Sloop Karena, and myself of the Leeward Eileen decided it would be unwise to try for Dun Laoghaire as intended, lying due west. There was a sporting chance that Port St. Mary in the Isle of Man would better suit our purpose.

At 1550 we dropped our moorings off the Gazelle Hotel in the Menai Straits, and ran down to Puffin Island, High Water was at 1635 which would give us the full ebb and flood for the crossing. The flood not being met till well clear of Anglesey. The breeze gradually dropped, but we were through Puffin Sound by 1745. The barometer had dropped from 30.3 to 30.2. Once through the Sound we found that we could not lay our course but the ebb kept the boats on track.

High Tea about 1900 hours, the skipper's favourite Italian dish "Rissotto". One of the crew, Alun Pritchard, refused as he had met his match in "Rissotto" on the Conway Cruise. Eifion Owen, the other crew, was game to try and ate most of it, but was to suffer later.

In the light breeze the Mystic went a mile or so ahead. To maintain our cruising speed the Seagull was started at 1925 at half throttle and stopped at 2110 when we had overtaken Karena, At half throttle she will motor for two hours at about three knots,

By 2125 the wind was freshening, and measured on the ventimeter was a good five. We put in three rolls in the main. The wind was coming round to the North West quite fast.

The Mystic caught us up. The nearest we now could lay course was some 50 to 55 degrees either side, and the wind looked like staying there, and possibly freshening further.

Wilf on Karena and I had a shouting match, and on Wilf's suggestion gave up the idea of trying to make Port St. Mary. It would be very tiring tacking all night in this weather. But the wind was now fair for Dun Laoghaire, and at 2155 we changed course to 273 degrees. By this time we were some 20 miles on the Isle of Man course, and the new course would take us well clear of Point Lynas and the Skerries.

It was a pity that we now had to plug the young flood to get past Point Lynas, The tide was neaps, only being 22.9ft. Even so it held us back. On the originally planned cruise we should have been off the Skerries at 2000 hrs, having used the whole ebb to assist us there on course for Ireland.

The midnight wind was a good force six. Point Lynas abeam. Seas rough and rather tiring. A small boat is kicked around so much.

Still in the red sector of the Skerries. With Point Lynas, the Skerries and South Stack flashing away, it's far from lonely. The blaze of Amlwch and steamer lights passing, puts one in mind of Piccadilly Circus.

Wilf reported my new navigation lights a resounding success with a brilliancy uncommon for their size. It must be the silver tape lining the interiors.

0210 hrs, and Alun takes the helm. Eifion had found "Rissotto" too much for him, and was writhing in agony on his bunk with his head over the bucket in the cabin. Alun was not very well either, but had quickly recovered. I had been rather hungry earlier on about midnight and twice asked Alun for a sandwich. Everytime he looked at the bread he felt most unhappy. By 0210 hrs. I was past it any way and had a piece of Kit Kat which made my teeth ache.

Even now I can clearly see in my mind's eye, Wilf's Mystic heaving on the port quarter in the waves of the night. Silent like a large fish turning, sometimes showing her bilge keel, like a monstrous fin, In fact she sailed herself for two hours with the helm lashed. Whoever was on watch, just sat in the hanging locker just inside the cabin. There's comfort for you.

I lay on the weather bunk in my oilskins and almost dropped off to sleep, when Alun shouted down that Wilf wanted a word with me. At our present rate we would not make the Skerries till 0500, and there would still be 55 miles to Dun Laoghaire, say 18 hours at 3 knots, which meant arriving in the dark. We were still reefed down, and considering the 15 ft to 18 ft. waves were doing very nicely. Wilf's boat alongside disappeared in the toughs up to half the height of her mast and more.

We decided to repair to Holyhead for food and sleep. A new course to take us well clear of the Skerries and the time to turn was set, and I retired to finish my doze, and since the wind was lessening, took off my oilskins (one gets so cold and clammy in them).

Eifion recovered a little and went to join Alun in the cockpit, to talk softly in their native tongue.

At 04.30 I went back to the cockpit, cursing the low headroom which makes getting oilies on a gymnastic performance. This made me feel ill, but a quick visit to the side, and I was immediately happy and hungry again. Alun was far happier in the cockpit doing something, but Eifion retired below again.

Dawn revealed a wonderful mass of heaving water. We were abeam the Skerries at 0550 and running to Holyhead, wind now down to a comfortable force four. We sat looking forward and talking when the stern lifted to a wave and kept on lifting, till we toppled over the crest and slid down on the back of this rogue monster of a wave, to see it rush off down wind.

Holyhead harbour by 0700. The peace of it. We tied to the shelter of the wall opposite the Yacht Club. A large breakfast of eggs and bacon, tea and marmalade, was eaten in the cockpit in the early morning sunshine. Then a glorious sleep till mid-afternoon,

SUNDAY

After our sleep, we walked round to where Wilf and his crew Connie, were just stirring, and all went for the inevitable cups of tea and the inquest of the night's happenings.

What to do now? It was Sunday and no time to get to Ireland and back by Tuesday. The only course left was to complete the circumnavigation of Anglesey,

Wilf (good at waking up?) was to call us at 0400. At 0415 on the Monday morning Alun woke everyone complaining bitterly that he was all wet. It was raining hard and he was in the quarter berth. "My sleeping bag's sopping". I grunted and tried to get down for a few more minutes sleep, after all it was very early and raining hard. Fortunately Alun kept on and on saying he was wet until I was forced into wakefulness. I dressed and went and shouted Wilf.

We had planned to be off South Stack by 0530, The forecast had been light airs only. At 0510 we cast off and ghosted out of Holyhead. Force one NW. On with the Seagull, and in fact it stayed on till 1130 when we reached Pilots Cove.

I took a tacking course, aided by the motor, for North Stack, reached by 06.30. It was neap tides, very light winds with the ebb, so took the inside course along South Stack, then set course to clear Careg Hen race. In fact course was set for Nevin.

Wilf also reluctantly put his motor on but had given North and South Stacks a clear berth as he was some distance behind and later rounding the Stacks.

By 0800 we were just off Careg Hen. The E.T.A for Nevin at this speed was 1350, which would leave no time for lunch there, so course was altered to 096 degrees, which allowing for the almost beam tide, should put us on Llanddwyn Island. The sun came out and with it all the blankets and sleeping bags for airing.

At 1020 bearings were taken which showed we were exactly on track, and these were not the usual cocked hat variety, but a four bearing intersection. Visually we appeared to be making too much northing, but there was no arguing with the plots. As an experiment we religiously followed our course almost to the shore to see where exactly it would put us, and ended up about 200 yards north of the lighthouse by 11.30.

Feeling rather pleased at this we dropped anchor inside the rock guarded Pilots Cove, only a few feet from the circular beach. After lunch we had a tour of inspection. The light on Llanddwyn Island is on the ground floor of the light house and consists of a lantern dated 1861 facing a bay window.

1400 and time to catch our flood to go through the Swellies. A delightful Force three put us at Caernarvon at 1505, the Swellies at 1630, exactly the recommended time. We were almost becalmed in the Swellies and rather worried by a tanker following however it passed us neatly to starboard. However, a motor launch towing a yacht coming from Menai Bridge attempted to pass to the wrong side of the steamer and very choice words were shouted down from the bridge. The motor launch determined not to repeat the error swung across our bows to pass port to port....

I had taken down the working jib and hoisted my home made Parachute Spinnaker or Gennie (I never can decide what it is). Wilf was some distance ahead, but with this big sail (making a total of 158 sq, feet comparable with Wilf's standard 155 sq.ft we eventually caught up. Once through the road bridge we asked Wilf if he wanted a tow? A race to the Gazelle Jetty was agreed. The wind dead astern about force three. Side by side we literally foamed along. Wilf sitting on his foredeck booming out his jib and myself on my foredeck to keep the Leeward's transom out of the water. Connie was at the helm of the Mystic. The two boats sluiced through the water side by side, first one then the other inching ahead to the great consternation and jubilation of the other. When we passed the jetty it happened to be the Leeward that was ahead and won by one length.

An excellent and exciting end to the Whitsun Cruise.

V - First Rock Trophy Poem

Some talk of index error,
And some of tidal set,
And some just blame their spouses,
Or charts not perfect yet.
Some find their rock unaided,
Or soft mudbanks to lie on,
Or they may be lured aground
By 'Famous Five' or siren.

But rocks are no shame in the Venturer's Club.
If you hit a rock, then no-one will snub
You, or try to make you feel small:
Oh no, gentle listener, oh no not at all!
Nobody here will cut you to size.
Instead you will find they will give you a prize!

Brave Jim Benn
Bold Jim Benn,
Vowed he'd be a man of men,
And with courage high, and heart so true,
(For a man must do what a man must do),
 Gently, without the slightest shock,
He parked his ship upon Cribbin Rock,
And there she sat on even keel,
As Swelly currents fast unreeled,
 Until she lay with ebb so low,

A giddy drop opened below.
The bow hung over the void on the right.
The view from the stern was a sickening sight.
But nothing daunted, did Jim flinch?
No, he moved not a single inch,
Until the flood was full returned,
And with courage high and heart that burned,
With pride he sailed her swiftly away
And vowed this was his finest day.
(But after, fearing someone's courage would slip,
He quietly changed the name of his ship).

John, John, Doctor John
Courageous skipper of Avilion,
Wanted to go from Gigha to Jura,
And short of time, he thought t'would be surer
Not to have to go all the way round,
Bit take a short cut through Gigalum Sound!
So what if there's rocks, there's no need to meet
A spot any shallower than just over six feet
(Provided, of course, you find the right place).
 Doctor John set off at a spanking pace,
And if it turned out that his aim was not true,
Well, nothing to fear, he'd carve his way through!
(A hope quite forlorn, if he'd paused to take stock,
For glass fibre is softer than Hebride rock).

The rain, how it rained. The wind, how it blew!
And Seamint's skipper said 'this won't do!'
That Scottish foul weather so rudely should snub
An ex-Commodore of the Venturers' Club?
'No this will not do, and for two pins
I'll make Bonny Scotland pay for her sins.
I'm sick of looking at rain and white water
A judicious chastisement is definitely in order.'
And so without saying anything more
He rammed his ship hard into Scotland's proud shores:
Oh Scotland dour, you've long withstood
Assault by fibre glass or wood.
But Scotland, now how does it feel,
For this time its a ship of rock
Reinforced with steel!

The sky went dark !
A terrible shock
Shuddered through Scotland's foundations of rock
Castles shook and in every town,
Tiles and bricks and chimney pots,
They all came crashing down!
The Cairngorms quaked, and more terrible still,
 Edinburgh castle slid from its hill;
Ben Nevis staggered to and fro
 Then crashed into the void below,
And finally, oh worst of all,
A chasm appeared along Hadrian's wall.
(Indeed it was a terrible sight,
For all of Scotland had moved to the right,

And at the same time, though some may be Peeved,
Devolution was also achieved).

So if you cruise to Scotland
Then you can be of cheer,
As long as Seamint is there too
The sun will be shining next year.

To Gordon, for services to Scottish meteorology.

JOHN POWELL

Index